DEDICATION

**Dedicated to babies on the go
and those who take them.**

D0517683

CONTENTS

3 PART THREE: BABY CLOTHES

4 PART FOUR: RECYCLING

5 PART FIVE: SIBLING GIFTS

ACKNOWLEDGMENTS

*T*o Rosebud Badour-Jacobs: One of the best seamstresses I have ever met! Thank you for your help on this project.

Also, thank you to the lovely mothers and their beautiful babies that were such wonderful models. The cute babies certainly bring the garments to life:

Mishell Rose with Nate Rose, 18 mos.
Emily Silliman with Carolyn Irina Shultz, 8 mos.
Rosalind Sully with Gabriel Walker Sully, 7 mos., and Theodore
  Hartwell Sully, 4 yrs.

INTRODUCTION

Congratulations! A new baby is about to enter your life or the life of someone close to you. We put together a collection of baby goods that are practical, innovative, and necessary for every mom and baby.

A complete baby shower (sewer's style of course) will be the talk of the town long after the baby arrives. Perhaps someone at the office is expecting a baby. A Mr. Stork goodie basket, filled by everyone at the office, makes a terrific gift.

On the go with baby? No problem. Create items from traveling high chairs to neck pillows and native-baby slings— our motto is double duty and heavy duty! The bassinet in a bag is perfect for going to Grandma's house and it will fit under the table at a restaurant or unobtrusively in a corner.

Looking for practical baby clothing with very few pattern pieces? In our designs, snaps are a must for easy diaper access. We even included some special preemie outfits for up to 5 lbs.

In all the excitement, don't forget the older brother or sister. The last chapter is a dedication to "Mom's little helper." We designed an infant-size baby gorilla that needs as much TLC as the new baby. The baby gorilla even comes with a car seat/back pack.

Pattern pieces can be found at the back of the book and on the enclosed tissue. These patterns require no enlarging!

SIZING & SEWING FOR BABY BY MAIL

Many people have asked me, "How do I know what size pattern to sew for a child that I haven't even seen?"

A simple, guaranteed solution is to mail a piece of Swedish tracing paper (see next page) to the parents. Ask them to lay the baby on the paper and trace around the silhouette of the baby with a pencil. Request that they also date the traced figure and mail it back to you. The pattern will look like a gingerbread boy.

When deciding on a size, simply superimpose the tissue pattern over the baby outline. This enables you to identify the correct size at a glance.

Remember, children grow fast! Consider how long it will take you to make the garment and take into consideration the time of year the baby will be wearing the garment. Go up a size if necessary. When in doubt, make the pattern bigger!

Take this whole concept one step further and create a baby-dress form. With this form you can "fit" the finished garment. Create this form by adding a 1/4-inch seam allowance to the traced baby pattern and cut out two baby pieces. Sew the two pieces together, leaving an opening at the side waist for filling. Stuff with fiberfill and slip stitch the opening closed. What fun! You are now ready to "fit" the clothes or determine if the baby will fit comfortably into travel-gear projects.

NEW ON THE NOTIONS SCENE

FOLD-OVER ELASTIC

Fold-over elastic is available in widths of 1/2 inch and 5/8 inch which are excellent for many projects in this book. This type of elastic is used in the garment industry for lingerie and sports wear and is now available to the home sewer. Fold-over elastic is available in black or white and can be hand dyed. It's fast to apply, easy to

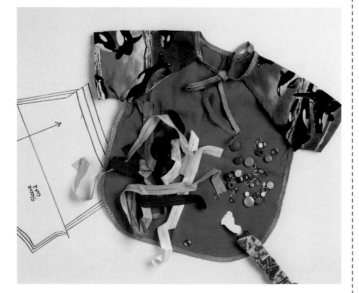

work with and never looks home-made.

SWEDISH TRACING PAPER

This tracing paper is literally from Sweden. Dressmakers use it routinely as they would muslin. It is sturdy enough to sew together and it will endure fittings. It can also be used to trace a required size of pattern. It is easy to make changes by tracing on the same paper as the child grows. The 30-inch width is convenient when working on larger pieces. Save your scraps. They are perfect for stabilizing embroidery or appliqué projects.

Swedish tracing paper also works as a pressing cloth! See *Sizing & Sewing for Baby by Mail* on the previous page.

SNAPS

Although snaps are not a new concept, attachment techniques have certainly improved. In the garment industry long-prong snaps are used to accommodate thicker fabrics. These snaps are also available to the home sewer. They are available in an array of colors or reflective materials for better night-time visibility. Two excellent devices for snap application include deluxe-pliers-type setting tools or a simple hammer device.

Snaps are a must for a child in diapers! If they are not put in, Mom will quickly discover the impracticality of the garment.

NOVELTY OVERALL BUCKLES OR SUSPENDER CLIPS

Buckles and clips are available in a variety of fun shapes and themes. There are no buttons to install and the strap slips through the suspender clip and clamps in place.

Enjoy sewing for the new baby!

Jasmine Hubble
Designer Mom

PART ONE:
THE BABY SHOWER

BABY SHOWER FOR EIGHT

When sewers throw a baby shower it's like no other! Instead of setting the table with disposable paper items we set it with real baby goods that Mom gets to take home. Right down to the invitations, you can do it all yourself or get friends to help. When the party's over Mom will go home with the following goodies:

- 3 crib sheets
- 8 Diapers
- 8 Burp rags
- 8 Bibs
- 8 Pacifiers
- 1 Receiving blanket
- 1 Stuffed animal
- 1 Door announcement sign: It's a Girl or It's a Boy!

Here's how to set your table: Cover an eight-foot banquet table with the 3 crib sheets. You may decide to place the center sheet crosswise. Tie the bibs to the chair backs with ribbon. Use the diapers as place mats and the burp rags as napkins. The pacifiers make great napkin rings. Use your choice of real dishes or paper goods, glasses etc. Type or write your guests names on the place cards.

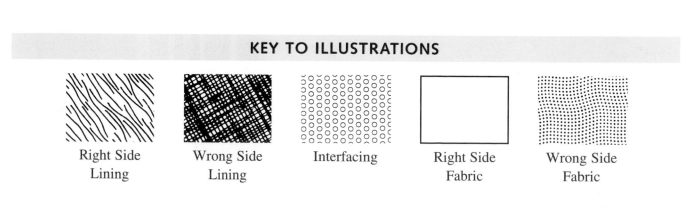

KEY TO ILLUSTRATIONS

Right Side Lining

Wrong Side Lining

Interfacing

Right Side Fabric

Wrong Side Fabric

INVITATIONS, ANNOUNCEMENTS

When you receive a sewn invitation in the mail like this, you just know you have been invited to a special event. They are as fun to make as they are to look at. This is a good time to use all those little odds and ends you have been hanging on to. Little pieces of elastic, ribbon, bows, scraps etc. bring these cards to life.

MATERIALS

- ♨ 8-1/2x11-inch card stock
- ♨ Envelopes size A2
- ♨ Scraps of fabric
- ♨ Matching thread
- ♨ Glue

BIB CARD

❶ Trace the card pattern onto the card stock and cut out, watching for folds. Place a square of fabric slightly larger than the front of the card over the front, right side out.

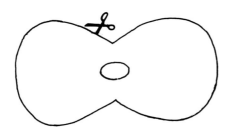

❷ From the inside of the card zig-zag around the outer and inner edges. Trim the fabric close to the paper.

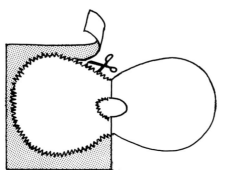

❸ Slip ribbon inside the shoulder at the fold and sew across to secure.

❹ Decorate with roses, ribbon, lace etc.

BOOTIE CARD

This is a bootie made from a stretchy fabric and the message is written on the sock.

❶ Cut out bootie and sew right sides together. Turn and roll down top edge.

2 Cut out sock note card and sew optional lace across the top using a zig-zag stitch.

3 Insert sock message into bootie and tie with a ribbon closed.

BASSINET CARD

This card works well for a christening.

1 Cut card out using the template in the back of the book. Cut in along dotted lines to fold card.

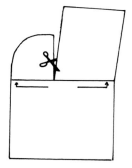

2 Cut pieces of lace extending beyond the edge of the card. Cut a piece to go vertical. Zig-

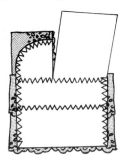

zag along edges and across fold to secure lace in place. Trim sides.

3 Decorate by adding a bow.

STORK BUNDLE CARD

This card not only makes a great baby shower card but also a terrific birth announcement.

You can choose flesh colored paper, use marker or watercolors.

1 Cut card out on fold and color.

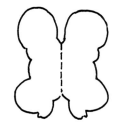

2 Cut a flannel square using the receiving blanket template for the card. Fold two opposite corners in and overlap. Wrap the card baby in side.

3 Tie a bow with some ribbon.

BIRTH ANNOUNCEMENT CARD

This adorable baby has a secret to share. Peeking over the top of a birth announcement, this makes a very original card. Could also be used as place cards.

1 Cut out baby from card stock. Water color front and back side.

Cut out a fabric diaper using the diaper pattern for the card.

2 Fold arms and legs as shown on template following the dotted lines. Use two small safety pins to secure the diaper.

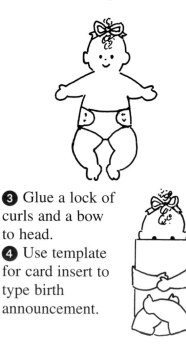

3 Glue a lock of curls and a bow to head.

4 Use template for card insert to type birth announcement.

SIX-FOLD THICK DIAPERS

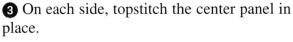

*T*he center of these pre-folded diapers are six layers thick! Before cutting, preshrink diaper flannel by washing in HOT water and dry in a HOT dryer.

SERGER TIPS *Use a four-thread over-lock with stitches set 1mm apart and 5mm wide. Round off the corners!*

MATERIALS

- 1-1/4 yards per diaper of 28-inch diaper flannel
- Woolly nylon in variegated colors to finish diaper edges

INSTRUCTIONS

1 Cut or tear diaper flannel into 36-inch pieces. Match selvage edges and press in half.

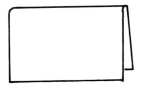

2 Turn diaper to position and selvage edge across the bottom. Fold the center of the diaper in thirds. Create a six-fold-thick middle section (divide by four and mark with pins).

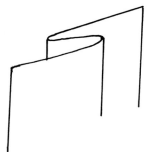

3 On each side, topstitch the center panel in place.

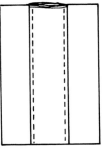

4 Serge around the edges using woolly nylon. The serger blade will cut off uneven edges and the selvage. If a serger is not accessible, cut off edges and clean finish them with an overlock stitch using colored thread.

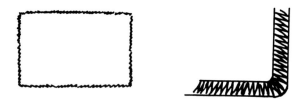

Option: You may choose to use decorative extra-wide double-fold bias tape.

BURP RAGS

MATERIALS

- 1 yard of flannel for 4 burp rags
- Cut out designs from other fabrics for appliqué (optional)
- 18-inch x 18-inch squares

INSTRUCTIONS

1 If you wish to embroider or appliqué the burp rag, then use a stabilizer such as Swedish tracing paper on the back side for stability. Tear away when finished.

2 With woolly nylon, serge around outer edges using a rolled hem, or make mitered corners.

3 To make the mitered corner, press the hem up into place. Press well. The crease lines will

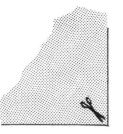

serve as guide lines. Make a small snip where the corner meets.

4 Open the pressed hem and refold it, matching the snips.

5 Sew from snip to corner where the pressed lines meet.

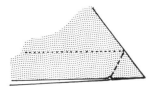

6 Trim back corner, fold and repress.

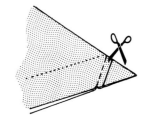

7 Decorate with colored pacifiers.

FITTED CRIB SHEETS

*T*his is another item you can never have too many of, and they are super fast to make. Standard crib size is 28 x 52 inches. Three crib sheets will cover an 8-foot banquet table.

MATERIALS

- 2 yards of 45-inch wide cotton, flannel, stretch terry, or knit for each crib
- 2 yards of 5/8-inch fold-over elastic

INSTRUCTIONS

109 x 172

❶ Prewash fabrics. Cut a 43x68 inch rectangle, making sure raw edges are square.

❷ Using the crib square template from the back of the book, cut away each of the four corners.

❸ With right sides together, close up the 4 corners.

❹ If you are zigzagging, press the raw edge 3/8 inch toward the wrong side. From the wrong side, zigzag the elastic covering the raw edge, pulling firmly on elastic. Overlap at ends.

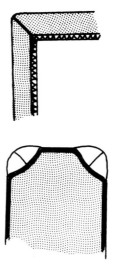

If you are serging, there is no need to press the raw edge. Serge the elastic directly to the wrong side of the raw edge, pulling firmly on elastic.

MR. STORK CENTER PIECE

Not only does Mr. Stork make a great center piece, but he also proudly announces: "It's a girl" or "It's a boy" on the front door once the baby's born. A full-size pattern is found on the tissue pattern in the back. He's much easier to make than he looks. Kids love to help color him and the place cards.

MATERIALS

- Three pieces of foam-core board 24x30 inches sold at office-supply stores and hobby shops
- Two 2-foot pieces of 5/8-inch half-round dowel for leg supports
- Spray adhesive or glue
- Sharp utility knife
- Orange poster paint
- Felt pens or markers: black, orange

INSTRUCTIONS

1 Glue two of the three boards together and allow to dry. Trace Stork parts on Swedish tracing paper. To save space on the tissue pattern, beak and head are separate. Tape them together to form one unit before cutting the board.

2 Trace one body on the double board. Trace the two wings on the single board. Carefully cut out the stork body and two wings with the utility knife.

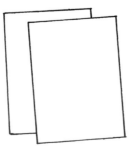

3 Paint the end of the wing feathers black. Make sure you have a pair, one left and one right.

4 Paint feet, beak, and leg dowels orange. Glue dowels to center of legs one at a time, allowing to dry in between

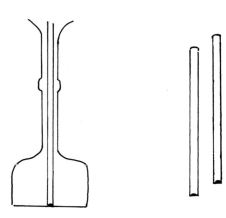

5 Glue wings in place.

6 With scissors, cut off the bottom half of a 1-gallon plastic milk jug.

7 Put Mr. Stork's feet in a ziplock bag, then place him diagonally in the milk jug.

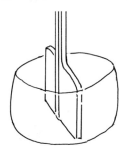

8 Fill with pebbles, rocks or other heavy weights.

9 For maximum stability, secure everything with string.

10 Fill with water and make an attractive flower arrangement to cover the jug. Ivy from your garden works well for this purpose. When all else fails, cover the jug with a receiving blanket. Tie ribbon to two corners of a receiving blanket and hang from Mr. Stork's beak.

For maximum stability, position the blanket close to his head. Slide a doll, bear, or dog in the blanket. If you still have room on the table, you can fill baby bottles with flowers. You are now ready for a sensational baby shower!

ANNOUNCEMENT SIGN
Trace the stork bundle onto colored paper to convert Mr. Stork to a door sign. One side will read "It's A Boy" and on the other side "It's A Girl!" If you already know the sex of the baby, then you're all set.

RECEIVING BLANKET

If you live in a cold climate, you may wish to double the thickness on this blanket.

We used a waffle-weave knit single layer for ours since we didn't want to add too much weight to Mr. Stork. Knits usually come 60-inches wide and they are easy to double up for extra thickness.

Cut blanket 30x30 inches. For

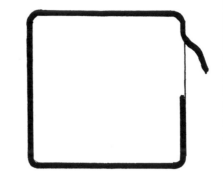

double layer cut two this size.

Serge around raw edges with

woolly nylon or use the mitered-corner technique as shown earlier for the burp rag. If you round off the corners, you can also use bias tape or 5/8-inch fold-over elastic. See resource listing.

TIP *Fold-over elastic is easy to sew on because you can take up any slack by pulling lightly on it. A 3-step zigzag is recommended.*

PLACE CARDS

If your kids love to color, don't forget to save this coloring project for them. If you plan to use the place cards outside, you may wish to place a small flower pot inside the circle of the card to act as a weight. You can even bake bread and serve it right in the flower pot.

MATERIALS

- Eight pieces of 8-1/2x 11 inch white glossy card-board or two pieces of poster board
- Colored paper

INSTRUCTIONS

1 Color and cut out name cards and staple together forming a circle.

2 Cut out bundles from colored paper. Hand letter or print guests' names on bundles.

3 Tape bundles on from the back side. Make extra bundles if you think the names might change.

MR. STORK GIFT BASKET

*P*erhaps someone at the office is having a baby! The Mr. Stork basket is a perfect way to let everyone at the office pitch in. The Mr. Stork basket can be loaded with all the little, important things the new mother will need but probably hasn't even thought of.

Most items are around $3 to $4 a piece. Loaded up, it's quite a valuable gift!

In your basket, you might include a bottle brush, bottles, baby-size fingernail clipper, diaper pins, pin cushion, diaper ointment, baby powder, lotion, rattle, bib, booties, socks, fresh wipes, electrical-outlet covers, cabinet locks, comb & brush, wash cloth, night light bulbs, pacifier, and formula.

MATERIALS

- White felt: 10x12 inches for head and 6x10 inches for wings
- One 6x10-inch piece of orange felt
- One 6x10-inch piece of black felt
- Polyester fiber fill
- An unsharpened pencil or small dowel for neck support.
- Two 1-inch eyes
- One white 10-inch diameter basket about 4 inches high

OPTIONAL LINING

- 1/3 yard of 45-inch-wide white cotton.
- 1/4-inch elastic or clear elastic.
- Hot glue gun and glue

CUTTING

- Cut two white stork bodies, two orange beaks, four orange feet, four white wings, and four black wings (see dotted cutting line for black wing).
- Tape head to body before cutting.

INSTRUCTIONS

1 Put beak parts in place using orange thread appliqué, one beak to each head. If necessary, trim white beak away from underneath.

2 Sandwich a small ball of batting between orange feet, then topstitch or zigzag together.

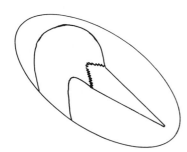

3 Overlay white wing over black wing and appliqué or zigzag to together. Repeat for other wing pieces. Use the first wing as a guide, but make sure you have two pairs when you're done!

4 Matching thread colors, sew the two pairs of wings closed. Leave an opening at the end for stuffing. Stuff wings lightly.

5 With the stork body right sides out, topstitch or zigzag just the beaks together using orange thread. Stuff beak only. Insert wings on sides. Sew from beak down across wings, leaving an opening between dots for stuffing.

6 Stuff head and beak firmly. Place an unsharpened pencil or dowel in the neck and stuff around it. Stuff neck firmly. Stuff body medium to light. Close opening.

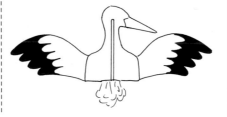

7 For optional lining, use a 12 x45-inch piece of white fabric. Sew right sides together, making a cylinder.

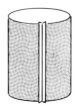

8 Press the top edge toward the wrong side 1-1/2 inches. Zigzag 1/4-inch-wide elastic or clear elastic over the raw edge. Pull firmly while sewing. Cut and overlap elastic at end.

9 Stretch and glue lining to inside of basket. (Clothes pins might come in handy to hold hot glue.) Position and glue feet in place. Place body at center back, wrapping wings toward front. Glue body to basket. Tack wings to handles. Add eyes with hot glue gun. Cut lashes from black felt.

TIP *Instead of a bow, use a crushed soda can painted with a baby face. Glue on curls and a paper pacifier.*

FINGERTIP TOWEL BIBS

When my kids were little I found myself favoring the fingertip towel bibs over all the other bibs we had. I noticed my husband did the same. As far as I'm concerned you can never have enough of these. They are easy to put on, cover a large area, have a high neck, and serve as a wash cloth when the meal is done. These bibs are so durable that 10 years later, we are still using them to clean the house.

Use your fancy embroidery machines to embellish them. You can purchase fingertip towels that are already embellished, or you can appliqué your own. If you are having trouble finding towels, make your own from yardage. You can also serge a hand towel after you have cut it in half.

MATERIALS
- Fingertip towel approximately 11x15 inches
- Neck ribbing 3-1/2x14 inches

INSTRUCTIONS

1 With the towel facing right side down, fold the upper edge over 4 inches. Find the center of the fold and mark with a pin.

2 Place the half-circle bib on the template, matching center marks on the fold. Cut away circle.

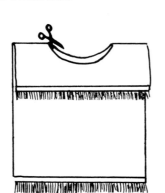

3 Close the short side of the neck ribbing. Fold wrong sides together and make quarter marks using the seam as one mark. Make quarter marks on the bib as well.

4 Sew the ribbing to the neck opening with seam at center back, matching quarter marks. Stretch while sewing. Add embroidery, embellishments, or appliqué.

PART TWO:
BABY GEAR

BED IN A BAG

When I had my second child, I wish I would have had one of these "Bed in a Bags." We were always on the go, running errands, and stopping places. This bed would have been the perfect resting place in between stops, or when leaving the baby for short periods with Grandma or friends.

MATERIALS

- 3 yards of 45-inch or 60-inch denim fabric
- 1-1/2 yards of 45-inch fleece, low loft
- 1-1/2 yards of fusible Perky Bond interfacing
- Nine pieces of plastic canvas approx. 10x13 inches
- 3 yards Supplex for lining
- 14x30-inch piece of mattress foam 1-inch thick
- Webbing for straps: 4 yards of 1 inch wide
- 1 yard of 45-inch stretch terry
- Eight extra-heavy-duty snaps
- 1/2 yard of 1-inch elastic
- Extra sewing machine needles for denim
- 8 yards of fold-over bias (optional)

CUTTING

Mark the following dimensions on the right side of the fabric following the layout.

- Bed Bottom: 15x50-3/4 inches
- Sides: 7-1/2x44-1/4 inches and 7-1/2x29 inches
- Side wings: Two 7-1/2x12-3/4 inches
- Flaps: trace two small and two large flaps from the pattern page.
- Pocket: 9x18-1/2 inches
- Five 2-1/2-inch bias strips (Omit if using fold-over bias)
- Fuse Perky Bond interfacing to the wrong side, covering all the above dimensions except for the bias strips. Layer Supplex face down, then fleece, then denim on top, right side up. Using safety pins, pin all layers together in several places inside the cutting lines. Cut out all pieces except bias strips. Eliminate fleece layer in flap and outside pocket

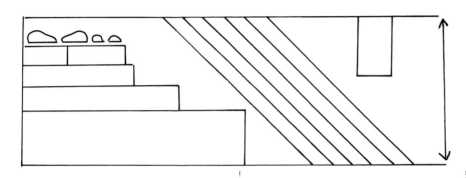

INSTRUCTIONS

Sew bias strips together to make continuous bias. Use a 1-inch bias tape maker and iron bias tape to make fold over.

❶ OUTSIDE BACK POCKET

Stitch denim and Supplex, right sides together using a 1/4-inch seam allowance. Leave small opening on bottom for turning. Turn and press. Insert elastic close to top edge and stitch across ends on outside pocket to secure elastic. Stitch again along bottom of elastic, forming a casing. Lay pocket on the right side of the denim fabric only on the bed bottom. Place top of pocket 11-1/2 inches from one end and 3/4 inches from sides. Topstitch across sides and across bottom, pleating excess on the bottom of pocket. Form a divided pocket by stitching 5 inches from one side, working from top of pocket to bottom.

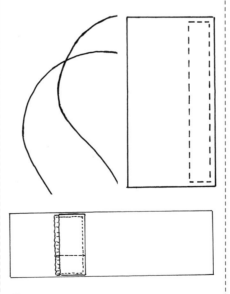

❷ BOTTOM OF BED

On the layered bed bottom, mark and stitch from left to right. The folding lines should be at 7, 12-3/4 (pocket section), 7, 12, and 12 inches. Insert plastic canvas into each section 1/2 inch in from side edges. If necessary you may join two pieces by using a zigzag stitch.

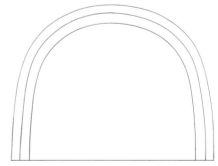

❸ WEB STRAP

Cut the 4 yards into a 3-yard and 1-yard piece. Insert the middle of the 3-yard web strap in the second 7-inch section 2 inches from the 12-3/4-inch section, between denim and fleece. This is necessary to support the baby's weight. Secure in place with two rows of stitching. Overlap ends 2 inches and stitch securely. Insert the overlapped ends in the last 12-inch section, 2 inches from the stitched line, between the denim and the fleece, taking care not to twist the webbing. Secure with two rows of stitching. Zigzag around all edges of the bed bottom.

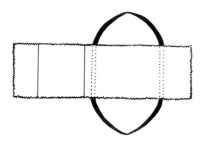

❹ SIDES

Undo the layers to join the side pieces, 44-1/4 inches and 29-3/4 inches, of the denim and Supplex with 1/4-inch seams and press. Layer with right sides out: denim, fleece, Supplex. Mark and stitch folding lines at 7, 12, 12, 12, 12, 12, and 7 inches. Insert plastic canvas into each section, 1/2 inch in from top and bottom edges. If necessary join canvas by zigzagging. Stitch a diagonal line from the bottom corner of the middle 12-inch section to a spot 7 inches out along the top. Finish side edges with bias strip. Cover raw edges of three sides with fold-over bias strip, mitering corners.

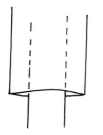

❺ HANDLES

Lay one side on top of the bed bottom, Supplex side on the inside. Match the stitched folding lines, raw edges even. Pin the web strap on an angle 5 inches from front edges of sides and 14-1/2 inches from the

back. Secure in place with two rows of stitching, stopping 1-1/2 inch down from top of side. Restitch webbing 1-1/2 inches down from top edge of bed with a 1-inch square with an X in the center. Repeat for other side. Zigzag side section to bed section.

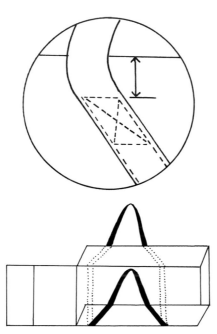

❻ SIDE WINGS

Layer with right sides out: denim, fleece, Supplex. Insert plastic canvas into each section 1/2 inch from edges. Cover raw edges of two sides with fold-over bias strip on one end and a long side. Topstitch along bias tape. Zigzag remaining edges. Join raw edges of the long side of side wings to bed at the 12-3/4-inch sections. Supplex sides together and stitch.

❼ FLAPS

Bind curved sections of small and large flaps, right side out, with fold-over bias strip, leaving straight side free. Stitch a small flap to the first 7-inch section of the bag. Supplex sides together, narrow end of the flap towards the first stitched folding line. Stitch Supplex side of large flap to the right of the first 12-inch section with raw edges together, large flap towards the 7-inch-stitched folding line.

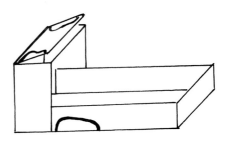

❽ FORMING THE BED

Join raw edges of the short side of the side wings to bed at the second 7-inch sections. Supplex sides together and stitch. The bed should now form a bassinet. Starting on the sides, cover all the raw edges with fold-over bias, hand basting in place. Basting will be necessary since it will be difficult to get all of this under the machine. Here is where you might break a few needles. It would be a good idea to wear safety glasses. Fold the end of the bias strip under. Topstitch along edges of fold over.

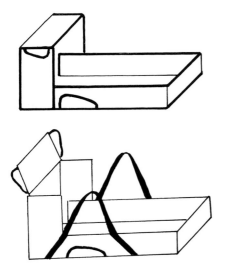

❾ SNAPS

Fold bed up starting at the foot of the bed. Fold on all the fold lines, tucking in the bag. Be sure flaps are on the outside of the bag. Use diagram to mark snap locations. Finish by setting heavy duty snaps.

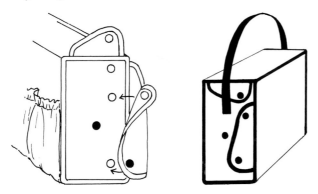

❿ CARRYING HANDLE

Carefully seal the ends of the 30-inch piece of webbing with glue or by melting with a candle flame. Fold under 1 inch and center 5 inches down from top on each side of bag. Securely stitch a 1-inch square with an X in the center on each side.

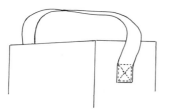

⓫ MATTRESS COVER

Cut Supplex 31-3/4x31-3/4 inches. Fold in half, right sides together. Stitch 1/4-inch seam across one short end and down the side. Stitch 2 inches on each end of remaining short end leaving an opening for turning and inserting foam. Turn and press. On the inside, stitch a 1-inch diagonal seam at the four corners (see bottom of diaper back pack). Turn right side out and insert foam. Close end by hand.

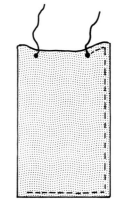

⓬ MATTRESS SHEET

Cut fabric 31-3/4x38-3/4 inches. Fold in half forming 15-3/4x38-1/4 inches. With right sides together, stitch 1/4-inch seam across the short end and down the side. Turn and press. Clean finish the opening by serging or turning a narrow hem twice. Slip sheet case over mattress, tucking the ends in.

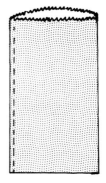

DIAPER BACKPACK

Manufacturers are finally realizing that moms are not pack horses. The trend has been smaller diaper bags. This diaper backpack really makes sense when on the go with baby. It's not too big and has a built in wipeable changing pad. It has two side compartments for baby bottles and plenty of room inside for extra clothes and diapers. We made ours to match our bed in the bag because we feel they both are the perfect travel baby gear.

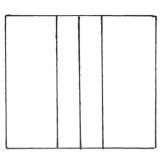

MATERIALS

- 1-1/2 yards fabric
- 1 yard interfacing
- 1/2 yard Supplex for lining
- Two quick-release clips
- One large snap for flap
- Two long-prong o-rings to match fabric
- 1 yard length of drawstring
- Eight large grommets
- 1/4 inch length of elastic or clear elastic

CUTTING

- Cut one backpack piece 16x26 inches and interface it. Cut one backpack lining 15x26 inches.
- Cut two flaps and interface one.
- Cut two pockets 12x13 inches.
- Cut two straps 4 inches wide, 36 inches long.
- Cut one snap tab 2 inches wide, 4-1/2 inches long
- Cut two changing pads (one from Supplex) 18 inches wide, 28 inches long. Interface fabric section of pad.

INSTRUCTIONS

❶ Sew straps and snap tab along the long side right sides together. Turn and press with seam running down center back. Cut one 5-inch piece off each strap. Cut snap tab in half. Push one raw end in on each snap tab and strap and stitch end closed. Sew two flaps right sides together. Clip curves and corners. Turn and press.

❷ From the wrong side, draw a line down the center of the pocket. Then draw a line 1-1/2 inches to each side of the center line.

❸ Press the top edge toward the wrong side 1/2 inch. Zigzag 1/4-inch elastic to raw edge, pulling tightly on elastic.

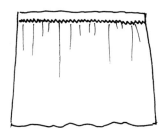

❹ Position pocket wrong side up on the right side of backpack even with the bottom and sides. Add one snap tab to each pocket, slipping it in approximately 2 inches down from pocket top, facing the outer edges. Stitch through the two lines (not the center one), backstitching at both ends. Repeat with second pocket. Stitch pocket closed and backstitch.

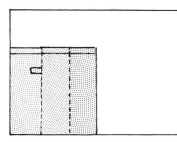

❺ Roll backpack up and fold pocket around roll so pocket is right sides together. Stitch pocket closed using a 1/4-inch seam. Repeat for second pocket.

❻ Press the top edge of the backpack toward the wrong side 1/4-inch, then one inch. Unfold again. Close the back seam of the backpack by folding it right sides to together.

❼ With pad pieces right sides together, cut a 1-1/2x3-inch rectangle away from the two top corners. Sew around pad leaving an opening at center top for turning. Clip corners and inside corners. Turn and press. Topstitch around pad from the right side.

❽ Pleat pocket bottom together even with the stitching on the sides.
  Baste pocket bottom together.

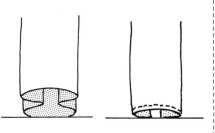

❾ With backpack inside out, place the changing pad inside with the wipeable surface facing the back of the pack and the sides of the pad folded over.

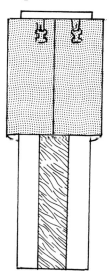

❿ Slip the ends of the quick-release clips onto the 5-inch pieces and fold them in half. Slip these tabs into the bag on top of the pad, and pin them 3 inches in from the raw edges sticking out from the bag bottom.

Note: Clips are visible in the previous illustration for location only! They are really located between the layers of pack and pad.
  Sew across the bottom of the backpack twice, stitching through pockets, pad, and tabs. Use a 1/2-inch seam allowance. Turn backpack right side out.

⓫ With right sides together, sew side of backpack lining closed. Refold with seam down the center back. Stitch bottom closed.

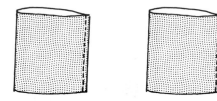

⓬ Pin lining to inside of backpack, wrong sides together. The raw edge of lining will be concealed under the pressed top edge of the backpack. Edgestitch around upper edge.

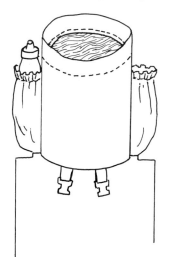

⓭ Position flap on the outside back of pack, even with the turned-under edge. Stick strap ends in flap at an angle. Stitch flap and straps in place, backstitching.

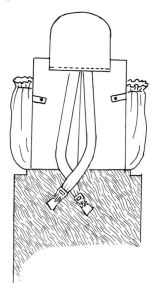

⓮ Slide the upper portion of the quick-release clips on the ends of the straps and adjust to fit. Set eight large grommets around upper edge. Thread drawstring through and tie closed.

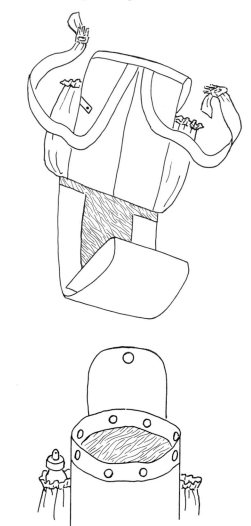

⓯ Set one large decorative snap, size 32, on front flap for closure and two open o-rings on snap tabs to hold pad in place. Fold pad and check the position for the second half of the snap so pad will snap to tabs.

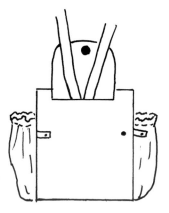

NECK PILLOWS AND CAR SEAT PAD

*C*hances are your baby will be taking his or her first ride home from the hospital in an infant car seat. Little ones will rest at ease with these comfy neck pillows in 2 sizes (newborn & toddler). Babies travel better and wake up refreshed with the infant car seat pad. It has a built-in neck roll. If baby spits up or gets sick, no problem! The whole thing goes in the washer! Choose bright cheerful fabrics!

MATERIALS

- 1 yard fabric for car-seat pad
- 1/2 yard fabric for two pillows
- Polyester stuffing

Note: For newborn size, use scraps. You can make the pillow two-tone.

NECK PILLOWS

*U*se 3/8-inch seam allowance and a 2mm stitch size (or one size smaller than normal)

INSTRUCTIONS

1 With right sides together, sew around neck pillow. Leave an opening between dots. Clip curves, turn, and press.

2 Stuff pillow firm, but not rock hard.

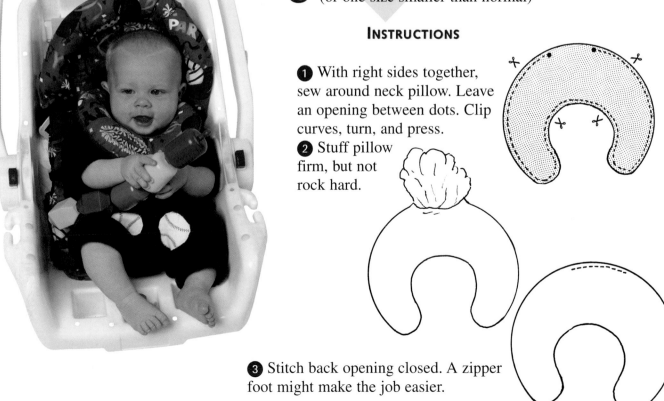

3 Stitch back opening closed. A zipper foot might make the job easier.

INFANT CAR SEAT PAD

*T*his infant car seat pad will help fill in the space between the tiny new baby and the car seat. The built-in head roll helps stabilize the wobbly head.

INSTRUCTIONS

1 Cut one neck roll 6-1/2x25 inches. With fabric right sides out, sew neck roll closed using a 1/2-inch seam. Stuff roll from both ends.

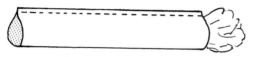

2 Baste neck roll to front pad piece, matching roll ends with seat-belt slits. Baste ends closed.

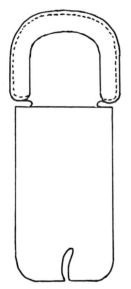

3 Baste the wrong side of the back seat pad to batting and cut away excess batting.

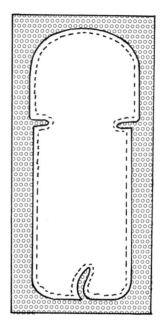

4 With fabric right sides together and neck roll on the inside, sew seat pads together. Sew around seat-belt slits and leave an opening between dots for turning. Clip around and in between curves. Turn and press.

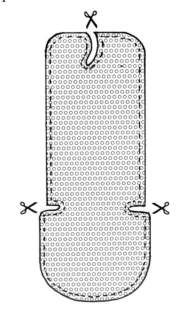

Option: Do a final topstitch around pad.

FLEECE BLANKET PILLOW

When you're out and about, this little pillow fits right inside the stroller and helps keep baby propped up. When it starts to cool down and you need to bundle up, simply unfold the pillow into a nice snugly blanket. Inside the pillow is a cap and a pair of fleece boots.

We put some fancy pearl rayon in the serger to give it the blanket-edge look. Set your serger-stitch length wider and closer together.

MATERIALS

- 1-1/4 yards of polar fleece
- Decorative serging thread or pearl rayon.

CUTTING

- Cut one 45-inch square for the blanket and one 9x14-inch piece for the pillow.

❶ Serge around one long and one short side of the pillow.

❷ Place the pillow in a corner so the unserged sides are matching the outer edges of the blan-

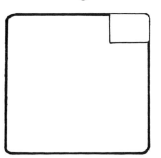

ket. Serge around the blanket, catching the pillow at the same time. Round corners are easier to serge.

❸ Fold blanket in fourths so it is the size of the pillow.

❹ Fold up from the bottom to the pillow, and then flip the pillow on top so just the pillow is showing.

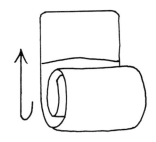

❺ Place your hand in the pillow and flip the pillow inside out. Turn the blanket to the inside.

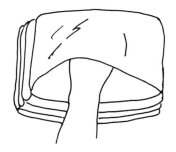

FLEECE CAP

*U*se the one-fourth oval pattern to make a full oval, then cut two full-size ovals from leftover fleece.

1 Sew the two ovals right sides together, leaving an opening towards the top for turning. Turn right side out and close opening.

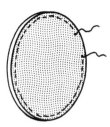

2 Pull the ovals apart and push one into the other.

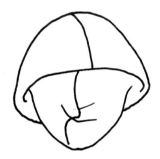

3 Flip up lower edge to form a cuff.

FLEECE SOCKS

CUTTING

- Cut from leftover blanket pillow. It is important that the greater stretch runs across the fabric rather then down.
- Cut two soles, two tops, and two heels.

INSTRUCTIONS

1 With right sides together, sew a sole to a top, matching center fronts. Sew from notch to notch.

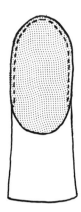

2 Sew heel to sole, matching center backs. Sew heel to top as well. Turn top edge toward wrong side 1/2 inch and stitch to form a casing. Leave a small opening to insert elastic. Insert 1/4-inch elastic and pull slightly to gather. Close opening. You may also finish top edge using fold-over elastic.

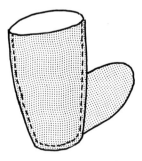

PLAY-QUILT TOTE

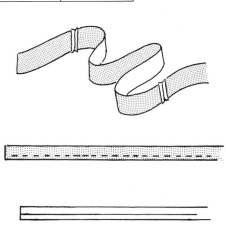

*A*nother great item when on the go with baby is the play-quilt tote. This tote opens up into a great play quilt, then folds and zips back into the bag. Of course there's room for play items as well.

MATERIALS

- 2 yards of a solid 45-inch-wide fabric for bag side
- 2-3/4 yards of a printed 45-inch-wide fabric for quilt side
- 2 yards of 45-inch-wide quilt batting
- 4 yards of 1-inch webbing for straps
- Two 18-inch nylon-coil zippers

INSTRUCTIONS

❶ To make bag side from fabric, press and crease bag side lengthwise and crosswise by folding in half.

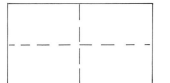

❷ With right sides together, seam zipper band together to form one long strip. Sew lengthwise, turn and press with seam down the center back.

❸ Interface zipper tabs with a scrap of interfacing. Fold in half and sew the two sides closed. Turn and press raw edges toward the inside. Repeat for second zipper tab.

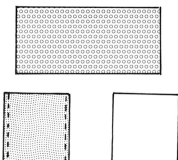

4 Stick the end of the zipper into the tab. Make sure the metal stopper is far enough down to clear the stitching. Stitch across the zipper attaching tab. Repeat for second zipper.

5 Pin zipper band, seam side down, along the lengthwise crease. Trim off excess.

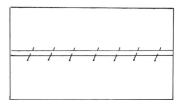

6 Open zipper. Pin one half to one side and one half to the other side with the teeth facing up. The first 2 inches of the zipper should remain free and the center of the zipper matches the center cross-wise crease.

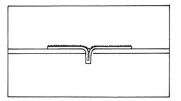

7 Flip the free end of the zipper out of the way and topstitch zipper band along the edge without the zipper teeth first. Flip zipper down again, and on the edge with the teeth, sew up to where the zipper is free, backstitching to secure. Continue on the other side the same way.

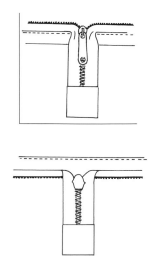

8 Fold pocket in half lengthwise and sew the short ends closed. Turn and press. Press in half to make a center crease along the short side.

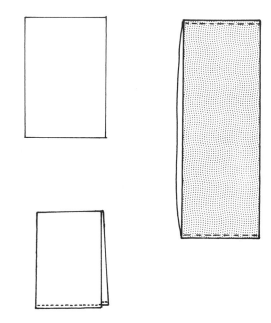

9 Place the pocket on bag matching center creases. Position pocket about 5-1/2 inches away from zipper band. Pin webbing over pocket starting at center crease. When you reach the top of the pocket, place a pin even with the zipper.

Measure a handle 33 inches long. Pin it even with the height of the zipper on the opposite side. Do this all the way around turning the end of the webbing 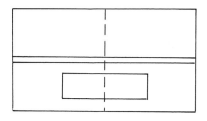 under 1/4 inch. With the pocket centered under the webbing, stitch webbing in place. Backstitch at ends and handles. Set bag side aside.

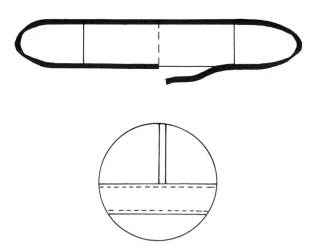

⑩ For quilt side or printed side, use 2 yards plus 2 inches. Square off both ends. Pin batting to back side. Bar tack by machine and tie with yarn, floss, or free quilt by machine.

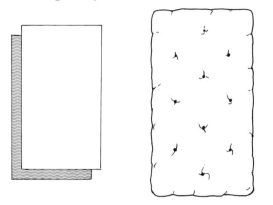

⑪ Place the quilt on top of the bag piece right sides out. With 1/2-inch seam allowances, baste all around to hold all layers together. Trim back seam allowances to 1/4 inch. Round off corners to avoid having to miter them.

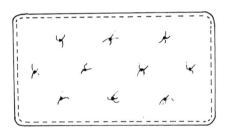

⑫ Sew the four strips of binding together to form one long piece. Press in half lengthwise with right sides out. Starting at the center side, pin binding to bag side with raw edges even. Underlap at the start so no raw edges will show. Sew all around the quilt.

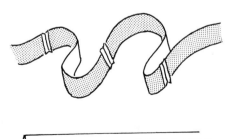

⑬ Pin binding to quilt side while smoothing corners. Press well. Open the second zipper and pin it in place in the same fashion as before, leaving the first 2 inches free. Sew all around binding, interrupting the stitches at the zipper.

Fold quilt, quilt side together, lengthwise. Fold the ends into the center. Zip the side zippers closed.

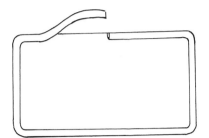

TRAVEL HIGH CHAIR

S ometimes we travel where a high chair is not available. Perhaps someone doesn't have children. Maybe their children have already grown up and a high chair is no longer part of their household inventory.

This little gem rolls up into its own carrying case with room for utensils and a bib. If an environment is not kid-friendly, you may choose to make a matching splat mat. Please never leave your child unattended.

MATERIALS

- 1-1/4 yards fabric
- 1-1/4 yards of Supplex for lining side
- 18" x 40" piece of batting
- 2-1/2 yards of 1-inch-wide nylon webbing
- Two 1-inch quick-release clips
- Bias tape
- Eight large grommets.
- 1/2 yard length of drawstring cord.

CUTTING OUT HIGH CHAIR

- Cut four waist straps, two fabric and two lining, 3-1/2x32 inches.
- Cut four shoulder straps, two fabric and two lining, 2-1/2x22 inches.

CUTTING HIGH CHAIR TOTE

- Cut one tote rectangle 8-1/2x17 inches and one pocket for tote 5x17 inches. Cut one grommet band 3-1/2x 17 inches and interface the entire strip.
- Use the bib-hole template from the fingertip towels in Chapter 1 to cut the circular tote bottom.

HIGH CHAIR INSTRUCTIONS

Sew waist and shoulder straps along the long side, right sides together, matching one fabric side to one lining side. Turn and press.

❶ Sandwich the batting between the fabrics with right sides facing out. Baste around outer edges 1/4 inch from edge.

From the lining side, pin shoulder straps and baste in place as shown. Pin fold-over binding (bias tape) in place all around catch-

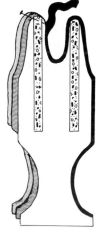

ing straps. Do not pin bias tape across the short ends!

② Cut two pieces of webbing 5 inches long. Slide lower half of the quick-release clip onto it. Fold webbing in half with clip in the middle and sew to lower part of high chair (see pattern for exact location).

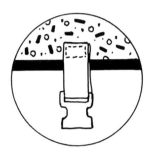

③ Cut two pieces of 12-inch webbing and slip an adjustable slider and the upper half of the quick-release clip onto the end and secure in place. Cut a piece of webbing 50 inches long.

Pin the 50-inch piece across the pad 1 inch below the curve of the shoulder straps. Slip the 2 longer straps, with the upper half of the quick-release clips on them, under this cross strap 5 inches apart at center with straps angling inward (see pattern for location and mark-ings).

④ Attach the waist straps on the side by extending it 1/2 inch

beyond the front. Stitch 1 inch from the outer edge. Trim the front piece (not the strap) to 1/4 inch.

⑤ Roll the strap to the front concealing raw edges of fabric and binding stitch in place.

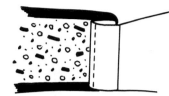

HIGH CHAIR TOTE INSTRUCTIONS

① For high chair tote, turn over the top edge of the pocket twice and topstitch in place or use binding. Place pocket on top of bag rectangle. Baste across pocket bottom and sides. Stitch utensil pockets by sewing through the pocket and tote 3, 4, and 5 inches from one edge.

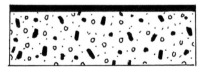

② With right sides together, close the side of the bag.

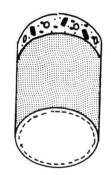

③ Baste the two circles for the bottom right sides out.

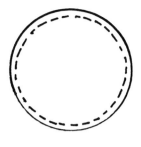

④ Close the short side of the grommet band and fold and press band right sides out.

⑤ With right sides together sew the grommet band in place to the top of the tote matching seams. Sew Circular bottom in place.

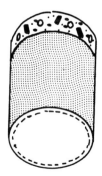

❻ From the right side, evenly set eight grommets for drawstring cord. Insert drawstring and utensils.

STORING THE HIGH CHAIR

❶ The high chair can be stored easily. With the waist straps folded towards the inside, fold the high chair in half length wise leaving the shoulder straps free.

❷ Roll up the high chair from the bottom.

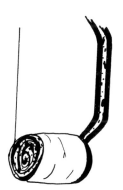

❸ Using the shoulder straps, secure the roll by tying up the bundle.

HOW TO USE THE HIGH CHAIR

❶ Place the high chair on a sturdy chair with rungs in the back.

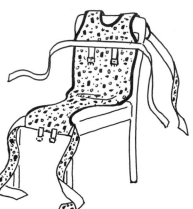

❷ From the back side, use the nylon webbing to tie the back in place.

❸ Follow with the shoulder straps. Thread them through the rungs of the chair and then tie tight.

❹ Place child on chair and bring up waist ties. Secure well in the back. Fasten child in place with quick-release clips. These are adjustable if necessary. Never leave child unattended!

I CAN FEED MYSELF BIB

*I*t's a major step forward when your children start feeding themselves. But look out for the mess! This handy bib includes sleeves and a front catch-all pocket.

Using fold over elastic you can use all your bright leftover fabrics and make stacks of them in no time. Supplex is a water repellent fabric that washes up nicely and holds back some of the messiness. This handy bib will fit in the highchair tote as well.

MATERIALS
- 1/2 yard Supplex
- 1/3 yard of contrasting fabric
- 1 yard fold-over elastic

CUTTING
Two sleeves, two pockets, one body.

INSTRUCTIONS

1 With pockets right sides together, sew across the pocket top. Turn and press.

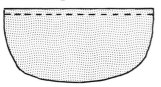

2 Topstitch across the pocket top. Optional trim can be used in place of this step.

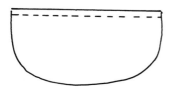

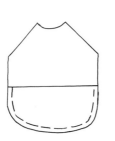

3 Baste pocket to bib body.

4 Press one side of sleeve down 1/4 inch toward wrong side, twice. Stitch in place.

5 With right sides together, stitch side seams of sleeves. **Note:** If you do not wish to put trim on the sleeve hem, then you may wish to hem it at this point.

6 Attach the raw edge of the

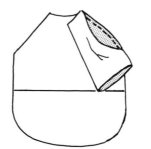

sleeve to the bib body.

7 Add trim to sleeve hem.

8 Starting from inside of the sleeve to the opposite side inside the sleeve, pin fold-over around the sides and pocket. Pull slightly while pining and smooth around corners. Sew in place using a 3-step zigzag. Cut a piece for the neck 35 inches long. Leave 14 inches hanging free for a strap and then pin

BABY SLING

*I*t's much easier to carry a baby distributing the weight across your shoulder blades and back than pulling down on your neck muscles! This design evenly distributes baby's weight utilizing the support of your hips as well.

This method of weight distribution has been used by natives for hundreds of years, so it must work. It's easy to make, easy to wash!

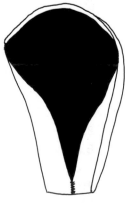

MATERIALS

❧ 2 yards each for side fabric and lining. (Choose a strong fabric such as denim or twill for the outside and line it with a soft flannel.)

❧ 36-inch length of string

DETERMINING THE SLING SIZE

To determine the correct sling size, tie some string together to form a circle. Cut string according to the size you think you will need: XS= 29 inches, S=30 inches, M=31 inches, L=32 inches, XL=33 inches.

Try on the string by crossing it over your shoulder the way you would wear the sling. When your knee is slightly bent, the bottom of the sling should just touch the middle of your thigh. Shorten or lengthen the pattern if necessary.

INSTRUCTIONS

Open fabric to a single layer and re-fold horizontally. Cut two slings on fold. All seam allowances are 1/2 inch.

❶ Place slings right sides together and sew around sling, leaving an opening between dots for turning. Clip curves, turn, and press.

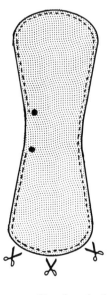

❷ Fold sling in half so the lining is on the out side. Sew the bottom closed using a 1/2-inch seam allowance. Stitch a second time for reinforcement. Back stitch at ends.

❸ From the lining side, press

seam open and topstitch 1/4 inch on each side for reinforcement. Stitch back and forth across the sides as well. Topstitch around the entire sling.

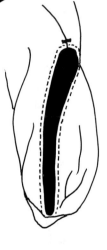

❹ From the lining side, find the center of the shoulder and fold outer sides inward, forming a giant pleat to make the shoulder narrower. Zigzag together about 2-3 inches.

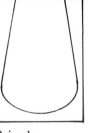

KANGAROO POUCH

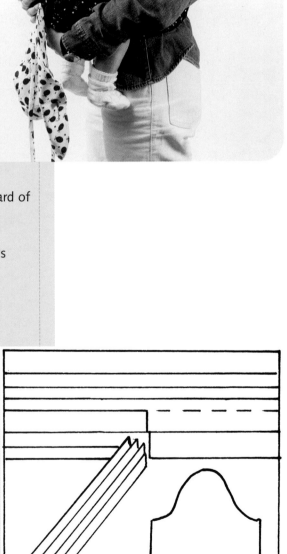

While Baby is still small, the Kangaroo Pouch is perfect for carrying in the front. A plastic insert cut from a 1-gallon milk jug serves as a great washable head support when sewn inside the head rest. The Kangaroo Pouch includes a back pocket for a pacifier and a front zip pocket for money or keys. It even has a snap-out burp rag.

MATERIALS

- 1-1/2 yards of 45-inch or 60-inch denim
- 1 yard fusible fleece or Armo-rite
- 1 yard Supplex for lining
- 1 yard fusible interfacing
- Quick release clips: three 1 inch, one 2 inch, one 2-inch slider
- Elastic: 3 yards of 3/4-inch elastic, 1 yard of 1-1/2 inch, 1 yard of 1/4 inch clear
- 7-inch zipper
- Two 3x7-inch pieces of foam 5 inches thick for shoulder pads
- Two matching open o-ring snaps
- 1-gallon plastic milk or water container

CUTTING

Fuse interfacing to approximately 22 inches of fabric before cutting straps.

Mark and cut straps as follows:
- Baby waist strap: one 2-1/2x36 inches
- Baby waist tab: two 2-1/2x4-1/2 inches
- Adult waist strap: one 4x45-60 inches
- Shoulder straps: two 2-1/2x45 inches
- Shoulder side tabs: two 2-1/2x7-1/2 inches
- Shoulder pads: two 4-1/4x17-1/4 inches
- Shoulder pad strips: two 4-1/4x8 inches
- Pockets: front security pocket 6-1/2x12-1/2 inches and 6-1/2x2-1/2 inches
- Back pocket band:1-1/2x10 inches
- Burp cloth: 9-1/2x8-1/2 inches (Cut one of Supplex and one of terry or cotton.)
- Burp cloth tabs: two 1-3/4x6 inches interfaced.
- Bias strips: approximately four 2-inch strips, the longest 30 inches

INSTRUCTIONS

❶ BACK POCKET

Press band in half lengthwise, press under a 1/4 inch on long edge. Stitch unpressed edge of band to right side of pocket top with 1/4 inch seam, press seam towards band. Fold band on fold line, wrong sides together. Pin the pressed edge over the seam covering the stitches. Stitch in the ditch from the right side.

❷ Stitch 7 inches of clear elastic to upper pocket edge, stretching elastic as you zigzag it on.

❸ Form pleats along the bottom, baste. Clean finish sides and bottom of pocket, press edges under. Topstitch into position on back of pouch.

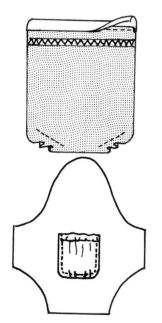

❷ SIDE SHOULDER TABS

Stitch long sides 1/4 inch seam, turn and press. Insert 1-inch quick-release clip onto strap. Fold strap in

half, raw edges together. Set aside.

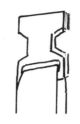

❸ BACK

Layer back and lining right sides together with fleece on the wrong sides of back and lining. Stitch side seams 1/4 inch, leaving opening between dots. Turn and press. Insert tabs into opening, stitch as shown. Topstitch along sides. Fold bias tape over raw edges of back, tucking ends in at sides. Stitch in place.

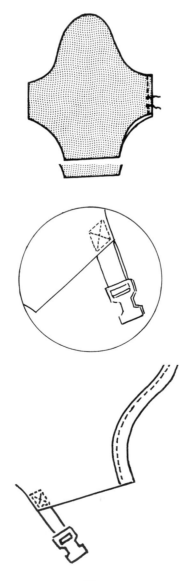

❹ HEAD SUPPORT

Using the curved side of the plastic gallon container, cut away the top and bottom of the handle section. Carefully cut the plastic with a utility knife. You can round all edges with scissors. Insert as shown, placing between the layers of fleece. Pin and then stitch around plastic.

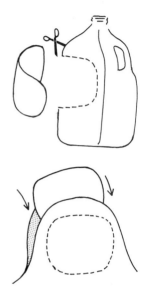

❺ FRONT

Layer front lining right sides together, with fleece on the wrong side of front and lining. Stitch side seams 1/4 inch. Turn and press. Topstitch along sides.

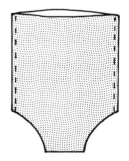

❻ FRONT POCKET

Press under 1/4 inch on the 6-1/2-inch edge of both pieces. Lay zipper face up under the pressed edges. Topstitch in place. Fold the long piece of the pocket, right sides together, meeting raw edges at the top of the pocket as shown. Stitch 1/4-

inch side seams. Cut off excess zipper ends. Turn and press. Position pocket on front, raw edges at top, topstitch sides and bottom of pocket.

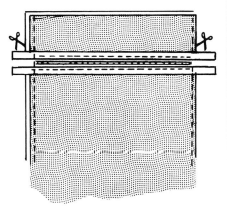

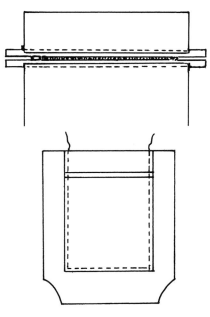

❼ LEGS

Stitch a 7-inch piece of clear 1/4-inch elastic to raw edges of back leg, stretching while zigzagging. Fold bias tape over raw edges of back and front legs, tucking ends in at sides. Stitch in place.

❽ ADULT WAIST STRAP

With right sides together, stitch long side with a 1/4-inch seam, leaving a 7-inch opening in the middle. Turn and press. Insert a length of 1-1/2- inch-wide elastic to fit your waist. Fold ends of strap in. Stitch, being sure to catch the ends of the elastic. Attach the slider to one strap looping the strap through the slider, the buckle and back through the middle of the slider. Attach the other end of the strap into the buckle. Stitch both ends securely.

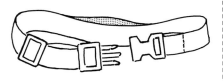

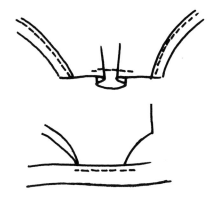

❾ CROTCH

Form a tuck on back and baste, stitch front to back at crotch seam, 1/4 inch with right sides out. Insert raw edges into opening of adult waistband. Topstitch in place, being sure to catch the under side.

❿ BABY WAIST TAB

Fold the waist strip in half, right sides together, stitching a 1/4-inch seam along the sides. Turn and press. Tuck the raw

ends in and stitch. Position on upper corner of side back at the edge of the side seam. Topstitch the upper and lower edge.

⓫ BABY WAISTBAND

With right sides together, stitch 1/4-inch seam along the long edge of the waist band strip, leaving a 10-inch opening in the middle. Turn and press. Insert a 27-inch length of 1-1/2-inch elastic. Fold ends of strap in. Stitch, being sure to catch the ends of the elastic. Insert raw edge of front into opening of baby waistband. Topstitch in place, being sure to catch the under side. Pass the ends through the side waist tabs to meet the center back. Attach a 1-inch buckle to the free ends of the waistband. Stitch securely in place.

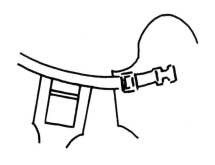

⓬ SHOULDER PADS

Turn the short ends of the shoulder pad strips over twice, 1/4 inch each turn, then topstitch. Position the strip 1 inch from the end of the 17-1/4-inch shoulder pad fabric. Stitch two parallel lines 1-1/4 inch apart, down the center. Fold the pad cover, right sides together. Stitch sides with 1/4-inch seam. Turn and press. Insert foam, tuck raw edges inside and stitch.

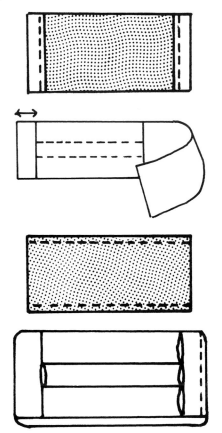

⓭ SHOULDER STRAPS

With right sides together, stitch 1/4-inch seam along the long side of the shoulder strap. Turn and press. Insert a 36-inch length of 1-1/2-inch elastic, pin one end. Insert the opposite end onto

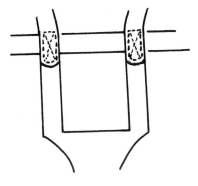

the buckle, fold ends of strap in, stitch being sure to catch elastic. With the strap crossed behind your back and the ends buckled at the sides, check the length of the shoulder straps, attaching the free ends to the front of the pouch on either side of the front pocket. Cut off excess length. Tuck raw edges inside, stitch. Stitch in place as shown.

⓮ BURP CLOTH

Round the corners of the burp cloth. Interface the top with a 2-inch strip on both pieces of fabric. Fold right sides of burp-cloth tabs together and stitch 1/4-inch seam along the 3-inch edge. Turn and press.

Position tabs at sides 1/2 inch from top edge of burp cloth, raw edges together. Baste in place. Stitch right sides together with a 1/4-inch seam, leaving an opening at the bottom for turning. Turn and press. Position a snap on the ends of the tabs and top of bib, wrapping tab around shoulder strap.

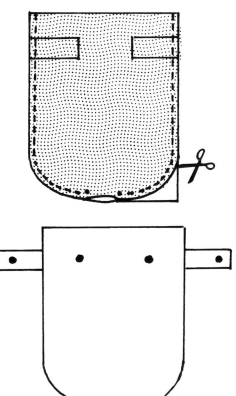

PART THREE:
BABY CLOTHES

With only a few basic pattern pieces, you can sew up a storm for the new baby. From layettes to practical, every-day clothing, you can mix and match all the components to create a whole new look each time. Sometimes a few pattern changes is all that's required to design a new outfit!

Note: *Unless otherwise stated, all seam allowances are 1/4 inch.*

ABOUT SIZING AND FIT

I mentioned earlier in this book how to select the correct-size garment. It's so important that I feel it's worth mentioning again. Everyone sewing has her own idea about how to size a pattern, and every pattern company is different. How many times have you heard a mother say, "My 12-month-old child wears a 2T?" The following sizes are to be used as general guidelines only.

NB= New Born
S= Small 3-6 mos.
M= Medium 6-9 mos.
L= Large 12-18 mos.

The proper way to ensure that clothes will fit the baby is to make a gingerbread-man tracing of the baby. It's worth it because you will get guaranteed results.

Lay the baby or child on some Swedish tracing paper and trace around the baby like a gingerbread man. Mail some Swedish paper to the person with the baby if they live far away. Superimpose the pattern pieces you plan on using over the paper baby to check for the proper fit.

It's easy and accurate.

Here's a list of the basic garment pieces printed either on the tissue pattern or on the actual book pages.

- Preemie layette / baby layette
- Overalls: long leg, cuff, or elastic
- Overalls short: with elastic or without
- Pants: long or short, with ribbing, elastic
- T-shirt with snap shoulder: short or long sleeve, with cuffs
- Romper: with or with out hood, short or long sleeve or leg, cuffs, ribbing
- Sleeper: same options as romper
- Diaper cover
- Lap shoulder T-shirt long, short, or sleeveless
- Swimsuit with baseball hat
- 3-piece jacket with hood / bunting bag

PREEMIE LAYETTE

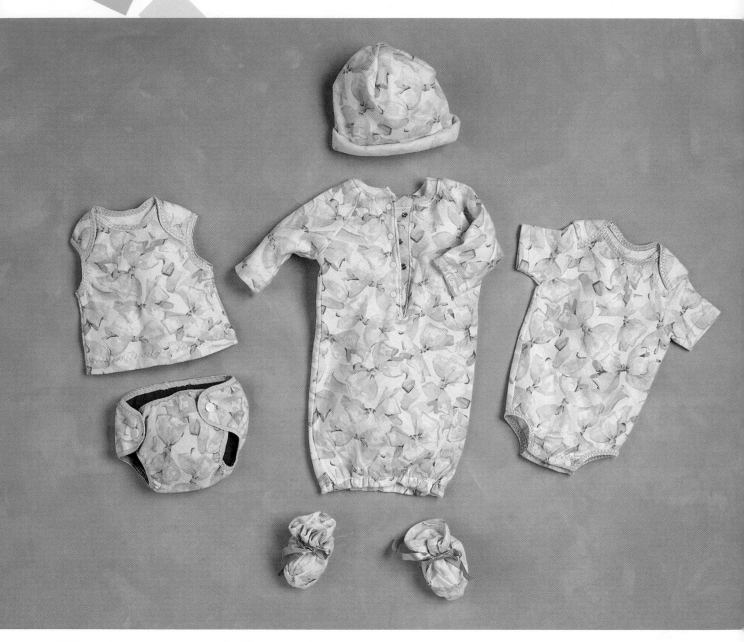

*I*f you have ever seen or held a preemie in your hands, you will agree that most commercial patterns are too big. We made every effort to scale down a few sizes running at approximately 3 to 5 lb. Preemie-size diaper covers are extremely hard to come by and they make up quickly. So, if you know a mom with a real little one, she'll be very appreciative.

Note: For regular baby layette, use larger pieces from the tissue pattern for snap-crotch T-shirts, T-shirt and diaper cover, and hat.

MATERIALS

- 1 yard of 60-inch-wide knits goes a long way
- Check your stash first for leftover knits
- Preemie-size snaps, size 7
- 5/8-inch-wide fold-over elastic
- 1/4-inch clear elastic
- Interfacing

GOWN

Cut one front and one back on fold. Cut two sleeves and one interfaced snap placket 2x13 inches.

1 Cut front open to mark. With interfacing together and raw edges even, pin placket to front opening, starting with the placket 1/4 inch beyond the top edge. Serge in place and end with placket extending 1/4 inch past the end. Trim excess.

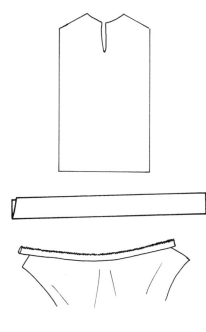

2 Press the placket flat on the left and then press the right side of the placket under. Topstitch around the placket. Trim excess placket away from neck edge.

3 Clean finish the lower edge of the sleeve and press a 3/8-inch and stitch-sleeve hem in place. Sew a raglan sleeve to each side of the front and the back.

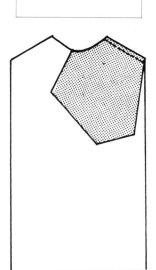

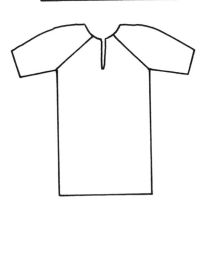

4 With right sides together, close underarm and side seams.

5 Serge or zigzag clear elastic to the wrong side of the lower edge, pulling firmly as you sew. Turn up hem and edgestitch in place or clean finish the lower edge. Press the lower edge toward the wrong side 3/8 inch. Edgestitch hem in place, leaving an opening to insert 1/4-inch elastic. Close opening.

6 Pin 5/8-inch fold over elastic to neck opening, stretching slightly. With a 3-step zigzag, sew fold over elastic to neck, tucking start and end under.

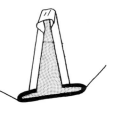

7 Set four or five preemie-size snaps (size 11-14) down the front of the snap placket.

PREEMIE HAT

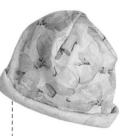

INSTRUCTIONS

1 Cut one on fold. Close side seam and the two outer angled seams.

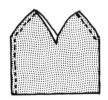

2 Open hat and refold in the opposite direction. Sew the remaining seams closed.

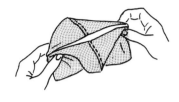

3 Clean finish the lower edge and fold up twice or bind with fold over elastic.

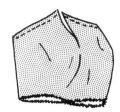

LAPPED NECK SNAP CROTCH T-SHIRT

❧ Cut one front and back on fold.   ❧ Cut two sleeves.

INTERFACE SNAP AREA

INSTRUCTIONS

1 Pin and sew fold over elastic to front and back neck openings, stretching while sewing.

2 Overlap back to front, matching notches at armholes. Baste in place.

3 Hem sleeve using a 1/2-inch seam allowance.

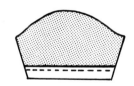

4 Pin and sew sleeves in place right sides together.

5 Close side seams and under-arm seams in one seam.

6 Pin and sew fold-over elastic to leg openings. Sew using a 3-step zigzag, tucking ends under.

7 Clean finish ends of snap tab on crotch. Fold interfaced-snap tabs toward the wrong side and topstitch in place.

8 With back overlapping the front, set three preemie-size snaps (size 7) at crotch.

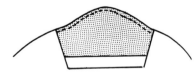

T-SHIRT LAP SHOULDER
(WITHOUT SNAP CROTCH)

*U*se pattern from snap crotch T-shirt eliminate leg area. Trace onto Swedish tracing paper and alter the pattern as follows. Straighten out the side seams so they don't taper in. Cut one front and one back on fold.

Sew same as snap crotch T-shirt steps 1-5 with short sleeve or steps 1-3 for sleeveless version. Hem lower edge.

SLEEVELESS T-SHIRT

*P*in and sew fold-over elastic to armholes using a 3-step zigzag. Close side seams.

Clean finish lower edge of T-shirt. Press up a 1-inch hem. Edgestitch hem in place.

DIAPER COVER

INSTRUCTIONS

❶ Interface the areas where the snaps would go with at least two layers of interfacing.

❷ Baste the two diaper covers together right sides out.

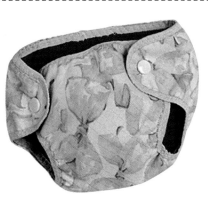
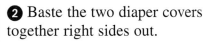

❸ Pin fold-over elastic to raw edges, starting at side front. Pin, smoothing around corners. At leg area, pull firmly to gather up leg area. Set snaps.

BOOTIES

Cut four soles, two tops, and two sides on fold.

INSTRUCTIONS

1 Sew sides together at center front.

2 Baste soles together right sides out. Sew sole in place .

3 Sew bootie top in place.

4 Hem top edge of bootie using a 3/8-inch seam allowance.

5 Add a ribbon and tie bootie closed.

SUN HAT

A Sun hat was added to our spiffy ladybug fabric snap-crotch T-shirt just to show that it can be worn as a sun suit.

CUTTING

⚓ Cut two brims and six hat sections and six hat sections for lining. Cut two chin straps 14x1 inch
⚓ Interface one brim section.

INSTRUCTIONS

❶ Sew brim seams closed. Place the two brims right sides together and stitch around outer edges of brim. Clip curves, turn, and press. Baste inner edges together.

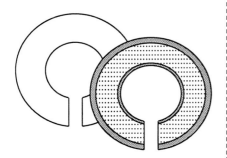

❷ Sew three crown sections together to form a half circle.

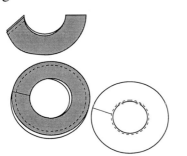

Repeat to make second half circle. Sew the two half circles together to make a full crown. Repeat if lining hat.

❸ Pin brim to crown right sides up and baste in place.

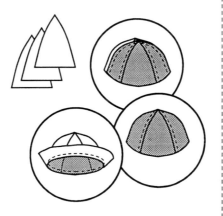

❹ Sew the long sides of the straps, turn, and press. Pin ties to crown and baste in place. Sew brim in place, catching chin straps.

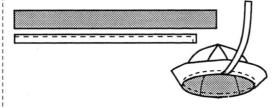

❺ Press edge on lining section toward wrong side 1/4 inch. Insert into hat wrong sides together. Baste in place and from the right side stitch in the ditch. Topstitch around outer edge of brim.

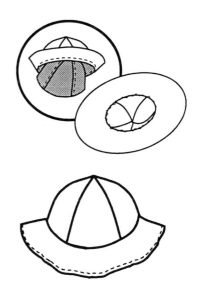

3-PIECE JACKET AND OVERALLS

*E*asy and fast to sew, this fun outfit is great to play in. The jacket and pants are only three pattern pieces! The jacket is reversible and has a water-repellent wind-resistant lining that can be instantly flipped to the other side. This jacket goes together in about an hour.

Note: The 3-piece reversible jacket pattern is located on the tissue. Our bunting bag is constructed from the 3-piece jacket pattern as well.

3-PIECE JACKET

MATERIALS

For outer shell
- 3/4 yards of 60-inch-wide fabric or 1-1/3 yards of 45-inch-wide fabric

For lining
- 3/4 yards of 60-inch-wide nylon Supplex
- 1/2 yard of 1/4-inch elastic for hood
- 3/4 yards of 1-inch elastic for optional jacket bottom

Note: Make all seam allowances 1/4 inch. Interface all snap plackets with a 1-inch wide strip of fusible interfacing.

CUTTING

- Cut one set for outer side and 1 set for inside.
- Cut one back on fold.
- Cut two fronts.
- Cut two hoods.

INSTRUCTIONS

1 With right sides together, sew fronts to back at shoulders and side seams. Repeat for lining.

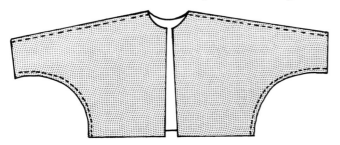

2 With right sides together, sew hood pieces together. Repeat for lining.

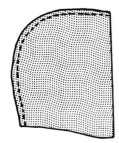

3 With right sides together, sew hood to jacket matching center back of jacket to center back seam on hood. The hood ends and starts about 3/4 inches from jacket edge. Repeat for lining.

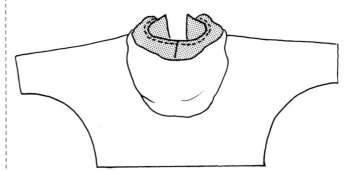

4 With the jackets right sides together, sew around hood down the front and across the bottom. Leave an opening at center back for turning and sewing sleeves. Clip corners and clip in by hood.

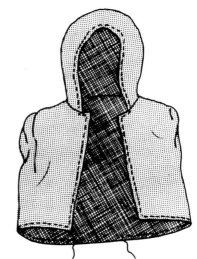

5 Turn jacket and press seams. Edgestitch around hood and then topstitch 3/8 inch away from first stitching. With a safety pin, insert 1/4-inch elastic and pull to gather slightly. Cut and secure elastic ends by stitching ends in place. You can stitch in the ditch by the hood.

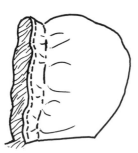

6 To bag the sleeves, press the 1/4-inch seam allowance on all sleeves toward the wrong side. Place the sleeves together as they would be when the jacket is finished. Take care that nothing is twisted and that sleeve seams are matching. Stick a pin in the seam allowances from the wrong side at the sleeve seam.

7 Carefully turn the sleeves wrong side out. Form a "bag" by having one sleeve go into the other, right sides together. Sew along the pressed crease. Repeat on second sleeve. Topstitch around sleeve edge from the right side.

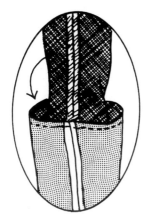

8 Topstitch all around jacket, closing center back opening. Topstitch front snap plackets by stitching 1 inch away from first stitching.

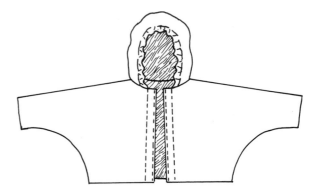

9 Topstitch lower edge twice 1-1/4 inches apart, leaving an opening to insert elastic at lower, center back. Gather slightly and secure elastic end in place. Close opening.

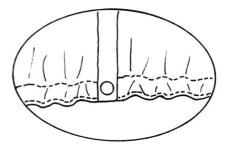

10 Even space and set four or five large jacket snaps size 24 or 32.

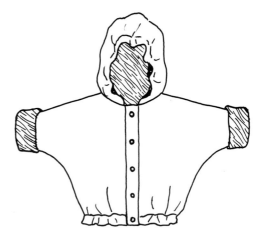

BUNTING BAG

*T*he Bunting Bag is great for riding around in the stroller or bundling up for a car ride. It is constructed from the 3-piece jacket pattern by adding a rectangular bottom to it. We chose a quilted fabric for the inside and dressed it up with the fur trim. Polar Fleece would work nicely, too.

MATERIALS

❧1/2 yard more than the 3-piece jacket

CUTTING

❧ Use 3-piece jacket pattern
❧For bottom rectangle: cut two fabric, cut two lining
Length times Height
S= 15x11 inches
M= 15-1/2x13 inches
L= 16x15 inches
❧ Follow jacket instructions steps 1-6.

INSTRUCTIONS

❶ Sew rectangles together at side seams on fabric and lining.

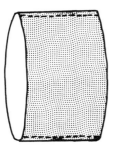

❷ Close jacket front and baste together to keep closed. With right sides together, attach the fabric rectangles to jacket bottom. Do not attach lining rectangle until step 8.

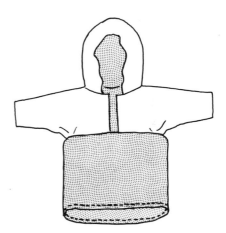

3 On the fabric side, sew the bottom of the bunting bag closed. On the lining side, leave the center 8 inches open for turning later.

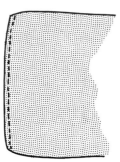

4 For feet room, square off the bottom of the bag by pulling the bottom apart.

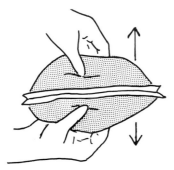

5 Sew across the bag ends 2 inches in from the end. Repeat on lining.

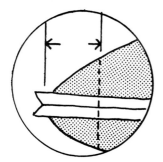

6 For optional fur trim, cut a 2-1/2-inch strip of fur for hood and a 1-1/2-inch strip for across the center. From inside of hood, pin fur piece and zigzag in place.

7 Roll fur toward outside of hood and sew in place by hand, covering zigzag stitches. You can insert elastic to gather up the hood by inserting it between the fur.

8 With right sides together, sew lining bottom in place. Turn through opening and close opening. Set five size 24 snaps down the front. We dyed ours to match using dyeable Anorak snaps size 24.

OVERALLS WITH CONTRASTING CUFF

*T*his pair of overalls has a contrasting cuff. The advantage is that the overalls can be worn a little longer because of the extra growing room.

PATTERN ALTERATIONS

This leg is designed for an elastic leg. Since there is no elastic in the bottom of this sample, the leg will be too wide. When you trace off your pattern pieces you must take away some of the leg width at the bottom by angling in approximately 1-1/2 inches on the inside leg seam only. Do this on both front and back of legs.

For the cuff pattern measure from the new leg bottom up 4 inches on the front and back leg and draw a line across. This will become your cuff pattern. Trace it as a separate piece.

MATERIALS
- 1-1/2 yards of material
- Suspender clips

INSTRUCTIONS

1 Interface front and back bib to fold line and 1 inch wide down front and back inside leg seams. Make all seams 1/2 inch.

2 Clean finish upper edge of cuffs. With cuffs right sides together, sew along bottom.

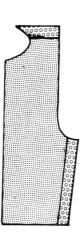

3 Sew center front and center back seams together. Press seams open. Clean finish inside leg seams.

4 Sew fronts to backs at side seams.

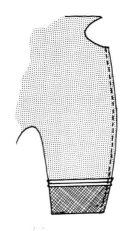

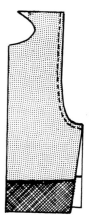

5 Open leg so side seam is running down the middle and cuff is wrong side out. Sew just through the cuffs. Turn cuffs right side out. Press the inside leg seam toward the wrong side 1/2 inch.

6 From the wrong side, top-stitch through the cuff along top and bottom.

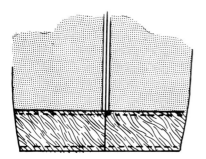

7 Fold bib right sides together and place a piece of bias tape over the armhole, overlapping the bib facing. Sew around the armhole.

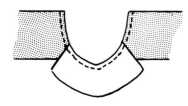

8 Turn bib facing right side out with bias tape. Press bias tape and stitch in place around arm-hole only. Insert 1/4-inch elastic in around armhole. Pull to gather up arm hole. Stitch to secure elastic ends in place.

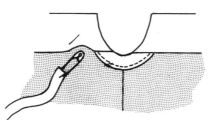

9 Top stitch around bib facing.

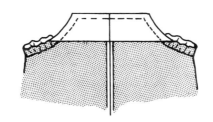

10 Cut two straps 2-3/4 inches wide and 16, 18, 20, & 21 inches long for sizes NB, S, M, & L. Sew the long side closed. Turn and press with the seam running down the middle.

11 Insert elastic 1 inch wide approximately 7, 8, 9, and 10 inches long.

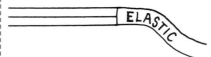

12 Secure elastic 1 inch from end. Pull and cut off excess elastic.

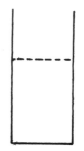

13 Insert strap through an over-all clip and fold toward the back. Stitch again to secure. From the opposite end, secure elastic in place the same as in the front.

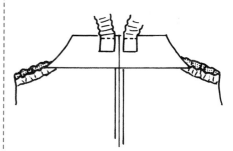

14 Sew straps to the inside of the back to each side of center.

15 Topstitch inside leg placket in place on both front and back. With front side up, install four snaps to each side of leg open-ing. Use long-prong open o-rings. The front should overlap to the back. O-rings should be showing as in illustration.

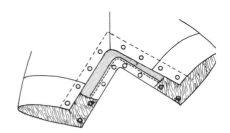

BLUE AND WHITE CHECK SHORTALLS WITH ELASTIC LEGS AND RED T-SHIRT

INSTRUCTIONS

❶ Use overalls pattern cutting on short leg lines. Sew and prepare same as overalls ignoring cuff instructions. Use 3/8-inch elastic in leg area.

❷ Double check to make sure front and back crotches are the same width. Trim to match if necessary and clean finish. Insert elastic through leg hem. Gather, but not too tightly. Secure elastic 1/2 inch in from both ends. Set three or four snaps in crotch. These overalls can also be done without the elastic and made to look more like shorts.

❸ The snap shoulder T-shirt was prepared using contrasting bias tape around the neck to match.

T-SHIRT WITH SNAP SHOULDER

Whether short or long sleeved, these T-shirts make up quickly.

MATERIALS

- 1/3 yard of 60-inch-wide knit
- 1 yard of bias tape or fold-over elastic.

CUTTING

- Cut one front on fold, cut one back on fold, cut two sleeves.
- Seam allowances 1/2 inch. Seam allowances around neck 1/4 inch.
- Cut 1-3/4 inch-wide bias tape from matching or contrasting fabric. Press in half right side out.

Option 1

You can cut the front and back with a 1/2-inch snap placket already added to the shirt. This is the fastest way. Iron interfacing to the placket as well as the shirt area under the placket. Serge the raw edge of the placket and turn it under.

Option 2

Add double-fold bias tape. This can be matching or contrasting. See short overalls with red T-shirt. Follow steps 1 and 2 below.

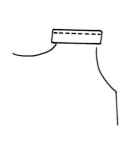

Option 3

Skip the shoulder snaps all together and have the T-shirt snap open down the front. Follow the instructions for the front from our preemie gown at the beginning of this chapter. See our white honeycomb knit outfit, long-sleeve shirt and pants with ribbing.

INSTRUCTIONS

❶ Sew right sides together using a piece of bias tape to the right front shoulder for a snap placket right sides together and raw edges even.

Option: This front placket can be pressed down toward the inside of the garment and topstitched in place. Repeat on left back. Do not topstitch placket down on back piece.

❷ With right sides together, sew the end of the double-fold bias tape. Pin bias tape to neck opening starting with the finished end of the bias tape flush with the placket, right side of bias tape to wrong side of neck, raw edges even. Press toward the right side and topstitch in the ditch.

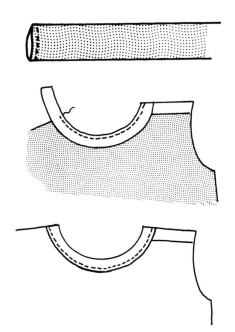

❸ Sew front to back at shoulder seam on side with no placket.

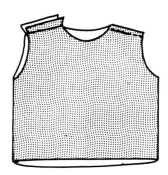

❹ Baste the side with the snap placket by overlapping back over front.

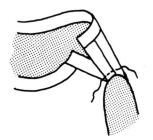

❺ Sew sleeves in place.

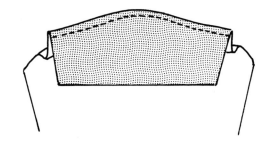

❻ Close sleeve seams and under arm seams.

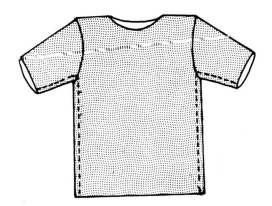

❼ Clean finish lower edge and press up 1 inch. From the right side, topstitch using a twin needle. Using a 1/2-inch hem on the sleeve, do the same.

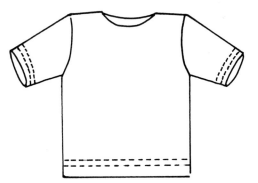

LONG PANTS

You can add a turned up cuff, ribbing, or elastic to the bottom of the legs for different options. For a great look that helps keep shirts tucked in, try adding elastic suspenders. Use flame-retardant fabrics for pajamas.

<table>
<tr><td colspan="2">MATERIALS</td></tr>
</table>

MATERIALS

- 1 yard of 45-inch or 60-inch material
- 2/3 yard of 1-inch elastic for waist
- Elastic legs (Optional)
- 1/2 yard of 3/8-inch elastic for legs
- 6 inches of ribbing (Optional)

INSTRUCTIONS

٨ Remember that you are making the pants longer by adding the ribbing, so if necessary, shorten the legs at the knee area.

٨ Use 6-inch ribbing to make cuffs. Cut length of cuffs the size of the leg opening minus 30 per cent.

٨ Decide on your leg options, then alter pattern accordingly. Cut two pants pieces from master pattern on tissue. See pattern alterations under overalls.

٨ Use sewing instructions for white long leg, long sleeve pajamas.

1 With right sides together, sew inside leg seams closed.

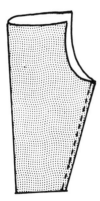

2 Turn one leg inside out. Place the leg that is right side out inside the leg that is inside out, matching seams.

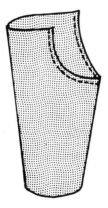

3 Sew around crotch seam like a horseshoe.

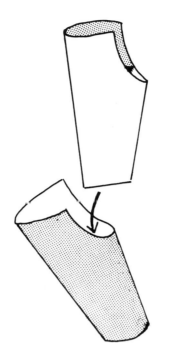

4 Clean finish waist and leg edges. For elastic legs and waist, press pants right side out. Press lower legs up 1/2 inch and the waist down 1-1/4 inches. Edgestitch in place, leaving an opening to insert elastic. Insert elastic with a safety pin and gather slightly so that the garment looks comfortable. Close elastic and openings.

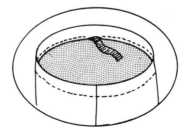

TIP *As a rule of thumb you take the waist measurement and subtract 1-1/2 to 2 inches. However, every elastic varies in the degree of stretch, depending on whether it is braided, woven, or non-roll elastic. It is sometimes better to eyeball it, especially on leg and arm cuffs.*

ATTACHING RIBBING

٨ Cut two leg cuffs 6 inches wide and the length of the leg opening less 30 percent .

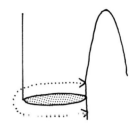

٨ With right sides together and the ribbing folded in half, close the short side of the cuff. Fold cuff in half wrong sides together.

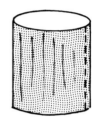

٨ With raw edges even, cuff seam matching inside leg seam. With right sides together, sew cuff to leg bottom stretching while sewing. Serge or use a small zigzag stitch.

SHORTS

⚜ For these shorts, you'll need 1/2 yard of 45- or 60-inch material

⚜ Our red shorts and striped doggie T-shirt will be everyone's favorite. The shorts were made from the long-leg pant pattern cut at the short-leg line and hemmed at the bottom of the leg. Otherwise they are sewn the same as long pants. Appliqué prior to sewing.

⚜ The T-shirt was made from instructions shown later in the book. Before assembling the front of the T-shirt, it was appliquéd with a cut out from another fabric.

⚜ Use cute characters from fabrics by ironing Wonder Under and fusing them to the front of garments. A satin stitch and embroidery thread makes it look very professional.

⚜ Don't forget to use Swedish tracing paper in the back as a stabilizer. Tear it away when finished.

PROTECTIVE SWIMSUITS

Since sunscreen is not recommended for babies younger than 6 months, your best protection is to cover them up. Our one-piece model snaps at the crotch and zips down the front for easy on and off. Our 2-piece model is just as practical and it's made from the same pattern pieces only there is elastic at the waist and no zipper down the front. The matching hat completes the outfit.

MATERIALS

⚜ Swimsuit fabric with at least 50% stretch in one direction and 100% in the other.
⚜ 5/8 yards of the main color
⚜ 1/3 yard of contrasting color
⚜ 9-inch nylon zipper
⚜ Strip of interfacing
⚜ Four o-ring snaps

INSTRUCTIONS

❶ On a strip of interfacing, trace the solid and dotted lines from the neck opening. Place interfacing strip on the right side of the front body section, straight down the middle. Baste in place to prevent slipping. Sew along dotted lines and then cut open along solid lines. Clip to corners at bottom.

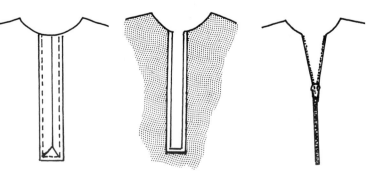

Turn interfacing to back side of garment. Pin and baste zipper in place. Sew using a zipper foot. Take care not to stretch while sewing. Trim away excess interfacing.

❷ With right sides together, sew side stripe to front sections. Repeat sewing back to side stripe. Close shoulder seams. Interface inside leg seams, both front and back for snaps, with a 1/2-inch strip of interfacing. Clean finish inside leg seam. Turn up 3/8-inch seams and topstitch in place.

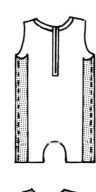
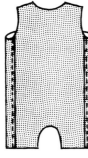

❸ With right sides out, fold sleeve in half along fold line and pin to armhole from stripe to stripe. Tuck under seam allowance on side stripe and sew sleeve cap in place.

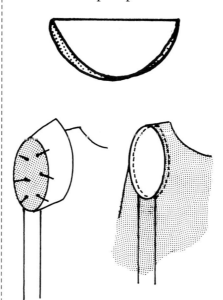

❹ Pin fold-over elastic to neck opening and use a 3-step zigzag stitch or cut a 1-1/4-inch-wide piece from contrasting fabric 14 inches long. Pin to the right side of the neck opening, allowing 1/2 inch to extend past the zipper. Sew in place. Fold neck band in half right sides together and stitch ends closed. Trim back seam allowance on ends. Turn right side out and sew neck band in place by zigzagging over the seam. Trim from the wrong side neck band if necessary.

❺ Hem legs by pinning a 1/2-inch hem. Zigzag or use a twin needle to sew hem in place. Set snaps in crotch area.

TWO-PIECE SWIMSUIT

*T*he same swimsuit can be made up into two separate units. Do this by cutting the pattern in half and adding 1-1/2 inches to each piece where you split it for hems. Repeat this for the side strip as well. Scoop out the front neckline so you can omit the zipper.

INSTRUCTIONS

❶ Sew side strip to front and back pants. Close inside crotch seam.

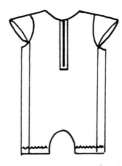

❷ Hem legs in the same way as step 5 in one-piece swimsuit. Make an elastic casing 1-1/4 inch at waist and use 1-inch elastic.

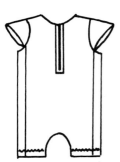

❸ Sew side strips to top and sleeves the same as in one-piece step 3.

❹ Hem top using a twin needle or zigzag stitch. Do the same as for legs. Clean finish neck opening. Turn under 1/4 inch and topstitch in place.

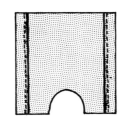

SLEEPER

*U*sing the romper pattern and flame retardant fabric, we created this sleeper which can also double as a play suit.

MATERIALS

- 1-1/3 yards of 45 inch-wide or 1 yard of 60 inch-wide
- Interfacing for snap area
- 9 inches of ribbing
- Six colored snaps size 16 or 18
- Twelve open o-rings for diaper area size 16 long prong

CUTTING

- Cut using romper pattern, shortening legs at the knee area by folding out 2 inches.
- Cut arm and leg cuffs 4-1/2 inches wide. Measure finished leg and arm openings, less 30 percent and cut ribbing this length. For neck ribbing, cut ribbing 2-1/2 inches wide. Measure finished neck opening, less 25 per cent. Cut neck ribbing this length.

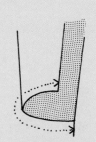

- Cut two front snap plackets 2-3/4 inches wide and 18 inches long. Trim to fit later.
- Interface the entire width.
- Cut two leg-snap plackets for front 2-1/4 inches wide and 10 inches long. Trim to fit later. Interface.
- Cut one leg snap placket for back the same width as front, but 20 inches long. Interface.
- All seam allowances are 1/4 inch.

INSTRUCTIONS

1 Press interfaced leg plackets and front plackets in half right sides out. On front sections, with raw edges even, sew leg plackets to fronts and backs. Make even at the top with excess at the leg bottom. Trim bottom to match. With right sides together, sew center back seams together. Repeat sewing longer placket to back leg sections.

2 On both front and back, from the wrong side, press placket outward with seam allowance facing inside of garment. From the right side, topstitch through the seam allowance close to placket.

3 For front snap plackets, refold placket right sides together and sew one short end closed. Trim and turn right side out. With right sides together

and even with the bottom, sew placket in place. Trim off the top to fit. Repeat for second side.

4 Press and topstitch the right front the same as you did on leg plackets. On left front, press placket toward wrong side and topstitch in place along both edges. Sew fronts to back at shoulders.

5 Attach neck ribbing as described in Romper instructions on page 70 under optional neck ribbing.

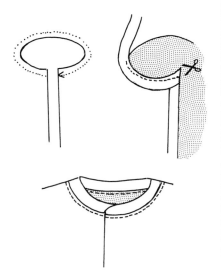

6 Sew in sleeves according to romper instructions steps 2 & 3.

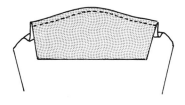

7 For sleeve cuffs, see cutting instructions for size. Fold sleeve cuffs in half and close the short side. Fold in half right sides out with seam on the inside.

Pin sleeve cuff to sleeve right sides together, raw edges even, and seams matching. Serge in place or use a small zigzag stitch.

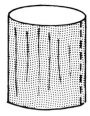

8 For leg cuffs, see cutting instructions for size. Interface both short sides of the cuffs with a 1-inch strip of interfacing. Fold in half, right sides together, and close short sides. Turn and press. Attach to leg bottom stretching while sewing.

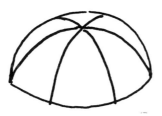

9 Set six to eight size 18 colored snaps down the front with bottom snap ending at placket bottom.

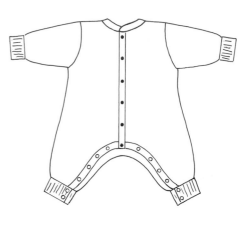

Set open o-rings to each side of this bottom snap continuing through cuffs. Set o-ring on back to match. Front leg placket snaps over back leg placket.

TIP *If you are working with bright colored fabrics it's a good time to use your leftover snaps. Use one of each color if you can.*

BASEBALL HAT

Cut six hat sections and two baseball cap brims.

INSTRUCTIONS

1 Sew three hat sections together to form a half circle, then repeat with the other three sections. Sew the two half circles together to form a full circle. Zigzag a piece of 1/4-inch elastic to the lower edge of one hat section pulling tightly. Hem the lower edge by a 1/4 inch, encasing the elastic.

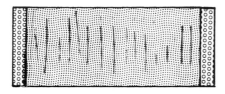

2 Interface both brim pieces. Place them right sides together and sew around leaving an opening for turning. Center brim in front of the hat under the hem. Topstitch in place. Use leftover fabric to make bows and dress up shoes.

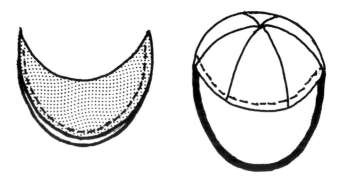

ROMPER

*T*his one piece is the most practical baby garment invented. It's great for playing in and great for sleeping in. Snaps in the leg area make diaper changing easier, and different options gives you unlimited additions.

Look at the options . . .

- Hood, hood with fur
- Neck ribbing
- Long sleeve, short sleeve
- Long leg, short leg
- Ribbed cuffs on sleeves and legs
- Elastic legs
- Turned, lined cuffs.
- Snap front, zipper front

MATERIALS

- 1-1/3 yards of 45-inch wide or
  1 yard of 60-inch wide
- Interfacing for snap area
- Reversible flannel for bear romper with companion bear

CUTTING

- For reversible model, cut two sets of everything.

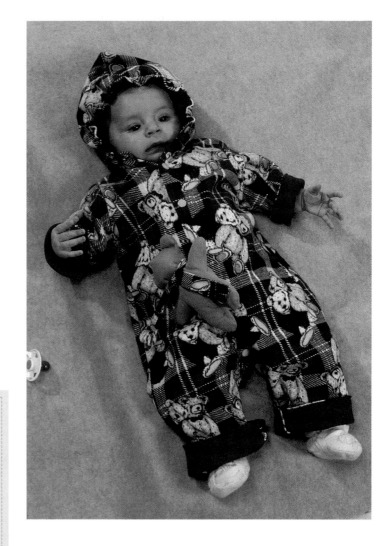

INSTRUCTIONS

- This model shows turned up cuffs in contrasting color. Follow pattern alterations on overalls with turned up cuffs.

- For snap reinforcement, interface center front openings with a 1-1/2-inch strip of interfacing on all four fronts. Repeat with a 1-inch strip in the leg area on same 4 pieces of fronts as well as backs.
- For ribbing at leg bottom, shorten the pattern at the knee by 2-1/2 inches to make up for the ribbing you are adding.

1 Sew center back seam. Sew fronts to backs at shoulders. Match center of sleeve to shoulder seam and sew sleeve right sides in place.

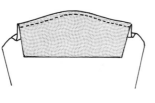

2 With right sides together close underarm seam and side seam in one. With right sides together sew hood pieces together. Attach hood to romper matching center backs right sides together.

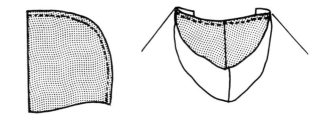

3 Place two rompers right sides together. Sew around the outer edges, leaving an opening for turning at the center bottom of one leg. Don't attach at sleeves.

Install 1/4-inch elastic in the hood the same as for the 3-piece jacket step 5.

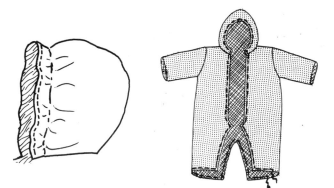

4 Bag the sleeves according to the directions on the 3-piece jacket steps 6 and 7.

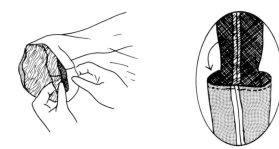

5 Topstitch around the whole romper from the right side. Set six snaps down the front and eight o-rings in the legs.

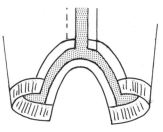

OPTIONAL NECK RIBBING

Measure neck opening, less 25 percent. Cut ribbing this length and 2-1/2 inches wide.

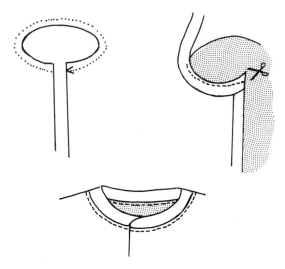

Fold ribbing in half lengthwise and pin it right sides together, raw edges even to neck opening. At start and finish, pull corner up so it starts from the lower corner. Trim corner and topstitch from right side.

COMPANION BEAR

- Cut one front and one back
- Sew head dart on front.
- Sew front to back leaving an opening for turning.
- Stuff and close opening.

PART FOUR:
RECYCLING
RECYCLED SWEATERS

*M*ost people have a bunch of sweaters in their closet that they just don't wear anymore. Perhaps one shrunk, another might have a hole in it, or there are some you just don't care for it anymore. No matter what the reason, they can be cut open into fabric and reused to make wonderful knitted baby clothing — without the time-consuming knitting.

In fact, these make up so fast with your serger that you might find yourself running out of sweaters. Second-hand stores seem to have a huge selection of sweaters any time of year. This red cotton sweater shown was purchased for $3.99. We thought it made a great Christmas outfit.

MATERIALS

- One sweater the length of your longest pattern piece
- One 12-14-inch zipper. Cut zipper off bottom to fit your suit
- Scraps for appliqué
- Woolly nylon for serger (Optional)
- Fur trim (Optional)

INSTRUCTIONS

❶ Cut sweater open along side seams and underarm seams. Spread sweater open so it lays completely flat.

❷ Lay large pattern pieces on front and back. If you are utilizing the ribbing from the waist-band, make sure you place the bottom of the leg flush with the waistband so it will form a cuff. Repeat with sleeve pattern on the sweater sleeve using the ribbing. Cut hood from leftover sleeve. Make sure you end up with right and left pieces.

TIP *To prevent fraying, avoid over handling the cut out pieces. Use woolly nylon in your serger and set the stitch width a little closer and make it a little wider.*

❸ Serge backs together at center back seam, right sides together.

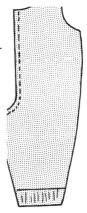

71
---

4 Serge fronts to backs at shoulder seams.

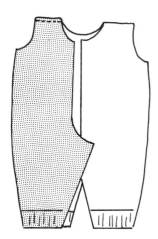

5 Pin and serge sleeve in place. With right sides together, serge underarm and side seams closed.

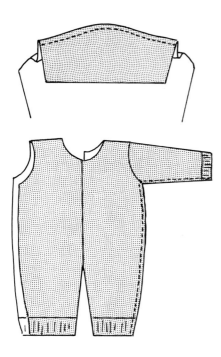

6 Clean finish opening down center front. Sew the center front opening closed from the bottom up about 2-1/2 to 3 inches. Pin zipper right sides together. Zipper tape side even with raw edge of front. Serge zipper in place without trimming

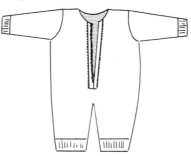

7 Close inside leg seams.

8 With right sides together, sew hood sections together. Attach hood to garment, matching center back seams. Wrap cut on facing from hood around zipper. Serge in place.

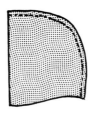

9 Press and topstitch hood facing in place.

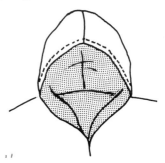

10 For optional fur trim, cut a 1-1/4-inch strip of fur to fit the hood. Zigzag along both edges of the fur, attaching it to the hood. Slip a cord between the fur and the hood. Appliqué optional. Ears are sewn right sides together and then turned for a 3D effect.

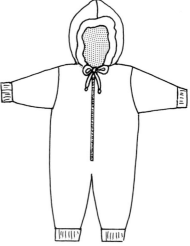

FUR-TRIM BOOTS

*M*ade from sweater leftovers, these sock-type boots complete the outfit.

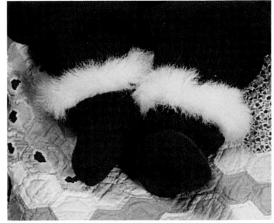

CUTTING

❧ Cut two soles, two tops and two heels.

INSTRUCTIONS

Note: It is important that the greater stretch runs across the fabric rather then down.

1 With right sides together sew, a sole to a top, matching center fronts. Sew from notch to notch.

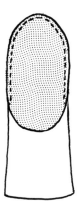

2 Sew heel to sole, matching center backs. Sew heel to top.

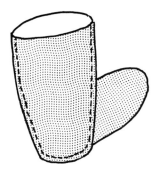

3 With boot turned inside out, place 1-inch-wide piece of fur trim, right side of fur to wrong side of boot, starting at center back. Edge stitch fur in place and trim fur to fit length.

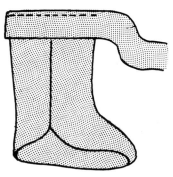

4 Turn boot right side out and flip fur down. Zigzag lower fur edge in place. Slip 1/4-inch elastic in through opening at center back on fur. Pull slightly on elastic and close elastic and opening.

T-SHIRT, PANTS, SUSPENDERS & CAP

Recycled from an adult sweater

Before you start cutting away, pin as many of the pattern pieces in place as you can. If it looks like you are running short, combine a second contrasting sweater or purchase ribbing if necessary.

MATERIALS

- One to two light-to-medium sweaters
- 1-inch elastic for waist
- 3/8-inch elastic for legs
- Novelty suspender clips
- Scraps for appliqué

CUTTING

- Prepare sweater as shown in the beginning of the chapter.

- For T-shirt, cut one front on fold, cut one back on fold, cut two sleeves.
- Cut T-shirt with cut on placket as shown in Chapter 3, option 1..
- For pants, cut two.
- Seam allowances 1/2 inch. Seam allowances around neck, 1/4 inch.

- When cutting front and back, cut a facing for the shoulder snap placket by adding a 1/2 inch. The largest size already reflects the snap placket.
- On the left front and the right back, trim away the snap placket. Interface the side with the placket and clean finish the raw edge of the placket. Press facing in place and over lap back over front with a pin. Baste in place.

INSTRUCTIONS

❶ Sew front to back at shoulder seam on side with no placket. On side with placket, overlap back over front.

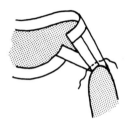

❷ Sew sleeves in place.

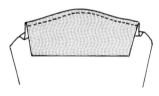

❸ Close sleeve seams and under arm seams.

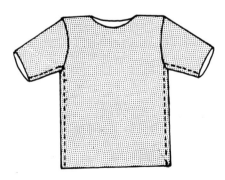

❹ Clean finish lower edge and press up 1/2-inch hem. Using a twin needle, stitch in place. Clean finish neck opening or sew bias tape or fold-over elastic to finish edge. Press and stitch neck in place.

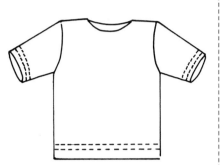

LONG PANTS

INSTRUCTIONS

❶ Use 1/2-inch seam allowances. With right sides together, sew inside leg seams closed.

❷ Turn one leg right side out. Place the leg that is right side out inside the leg that is inside out, matching seams.

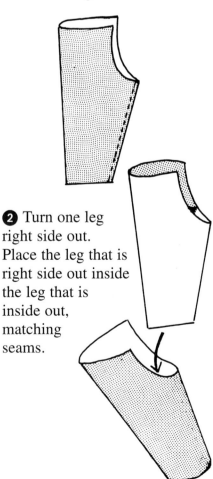

❸ Sew around crotch seam like a horseshoe.

❹ With pants right side out,

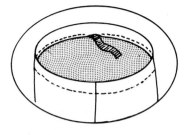

press lower legs up 1/2 inch and the waist 1-1/4 inches. Edgestitch in place, leaving an opening to insert elastic. Insert elastic with a safety pin and gather slightly so that the garment looks comfortable. Close elastic and openings.

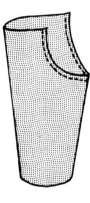

SUSPENDERS

❧ Cut two suspenders 2-1/2 inches wide. Sew long side closed, turn and insert elastic.

❧ Check length before cutting excess off. Insert elastic and finish as overalls.

CAP

This cap is nothing more than the end of the sleeve from the sweater. The cap was gathered at the wrist cuff. The other end was serged and then flipped up. You may need to make a band if you run short of material.

DAD'S OLD SHIRT

Shirts and blouses that button down the front make great jumpshirts. They involve minimal sewing time and work up into comfortable clothing. You will be required to do some serious eyeballing on this project. The paper gingerbread man method works the best as described in the beginning of Chapter 3.

MATERIALS

- Shirt or blouse
- Snaps for diaper area
- Gingerbread man tracing of child

CUTTING

1 Lay shirt flat on work surface, buttons face up. Cut the bottom of the shirt even if necessary.

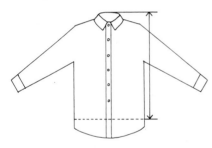

2 Place the paper baby on top of the shirt and determine how much to cut away for the crotch and legs. Mark the area to cut away with a disappearing marker. Cut 1-1/2 inches away from the actual legs. If the legs are too long, shorten the shirt some more.

3 Shorten the sleeves to fit the paper baby's sleeve length. If you are adding a cuff to the end of the sleeve, cut it by that amount shorter.

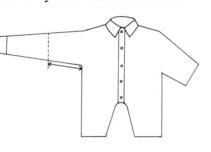

4 The shirt will be too wide and you will want to take away some of the fullness. Use the armpit as a reference of how far to go in on the side.

Do not cut too close to the body! Cut 1-1/2 inches away!

SEWING

Serge the underarm seams and side seams closed. You can close crotch seam by removing the last button if it interferes. Interface and clean finish crotch area for snap installation. Follow directions on overalls for snap installation.

For cuffs, see Chapter 3 for closed leg with cuffs and for snap crotch.

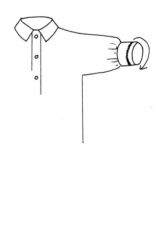

BATH LAYETTE MADE FROM TOWELS

*T*wo bath towels will make the perfect bath layette including one hooded robe, wash mitt, wash cloth, and hair towel. The embroidered bands give it the designer look. At $4.99, this is a better bargain then fabric! Since you wrap them and dry them in the robe, it will fit a baby up to 2 years!

MATERIALS

§ Two 24x46-inch bath towels

TIP *Use ballpoint needles when sewing on terry toweling.*

INSTRUCTIONS

1 Fold one towel in half crosswise. Using the Bib hole template, remove the neck. From the center bottom, cut the front open only up to the neck.

2 From the second towel, cut an 11-inch strip off one end for the hood. From the opposite end, cut off a 6-1/2-inch strip for the sleeves.

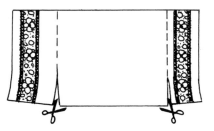

3 Fold in half and round off the upper corner about 2 inches. With right sides together, sew the hood.

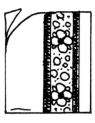

4 Attach the hood to the jacket using a 1/2-inch seam. Trim back the jacket side of the seam allowance to 1/4 inch. Utilizing the bound edge of the towel, stitch down the hood seam allowance, covering the raw edge.

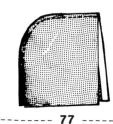

5 Clean finish the outer edges of the front opening and around the hood. Press back 1/2-inch placket and topstitch in place.

6 Because the robe is too wide, cut away 3 inches from the back side. Cut the front to match.

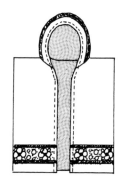

7 Cut the sleeve strip in half. Find the center of the shoulder and serge the sleeves to each side. Use the bound edge as the sleeve hem.

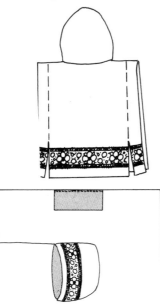

8 With right sides together, close underarm seams and side seams at the same time.

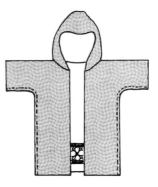

9 From the remaining towel, cut a wash cloth 7x8 inches and a hair towel 20x24 inches. Serge around the raw edges using woolly nylon.

WASH MITT

*U*se the pattern from the back of the book. Cut two mitts 5x6 inches from the remainder of the towel.

INSTRUCTIONS

1 Serge the two mitt pieces together using woolly nylon.

2 Cut two pieces of ribbing for mitt cuff 5x8 inches. With right sides together, sew the short ends of the ribbing closed. Fold in half with seam on the inside and make quarter marks. Repeat quarter marks on mitt.

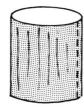

3 With raw edges even, attach ribbing to mitt, stretching while sewing.

CHRISTENING GOWN OR JUMPSUIT
RECYCLED FROM A WEDDING DRESS

*C*alling all grandmas! If you are thinking about sewing your child's christening gown, and your wedding dress is still in that box in the attic, now's your chance to cut it into an heirloom christening gown for your new grandchild.

We have the traditional christening gown complete with bonnet and booties, or it could be a pantsuit version for a boy. While your up in the attic looking, around for other family heirlooms that can be incorporated into this gown such as Great Grandma's hand-tatted handkerchief, mom's communion veil, prayer book covers, etc. For a lining, you can use one of Dad's white shirts. It will be special for generations to come.

MATERIALS
- One long wedding dress (will make approximately two christening gowns and one pantsuit)
- Other heirloom pieces such as handkerchiefs, veils, lace
- Dad's white shirt for lining

PREPARATION
- Examine the dress for wear and tear, especially in the train area. Use new lace and tea dye if necessary to cover any defects.
- If the dress has a bodice, detach it from the skirt first. If there is a lot of detailing on the back of the skirt you may use it for the front of the gown. Consider using scalloped edges as the hem on the new gown. Save bead work for in the bodice.
- Cut 1 gown piece 60 to 64 inches wide and 31 inches long. Other pattern pieces are located on tissue.
- Make all seams 1/4 inch.

GOWN

❶ BODICE

Fuse a 1-inch strip of interfacing to bodice and lining at center backs. With right sides together, stitch front to backs at shoulders on gown bodice and lining. Press. With right sides together, stitch bodice to lining around neck and center back. Turn and press. Understitch seam allowance to lining. Baste around armhole openings.

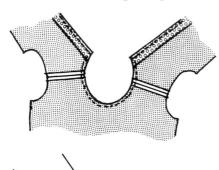

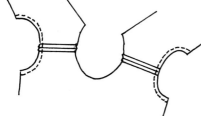

❷ SLEEVES

If necessary, hem the lower edge of the sleeve by turning the raw edge under twice 1/8 inch, or lay a piece of lace from the dress along the sleeve edge and topstitch in place.

If the lace is quite wide, you may cut away the sleeve fabric from under the lace. On the wrong side of the fabric, measure approximately 1-1/2 from finished edge of the sleeve and mark a line with a fabric pencil.

Using clear elastic and a medium zigzag stitch, anchor elastic at one edge of sleeve. Stretch 6 inches of elastic to opposite sleeve edge and continue to stretch while zigzagging.

Repeat for second sleeve.

Gather top of sleeve edge between notches. Pin sleeve to armhole, right sides together, matching notches on front and back and underarm seam edges. Stitch sleeve in place. With right sides together, stitch underarm and bodice side seams.

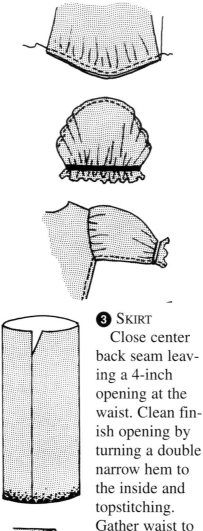

❸ SKIRT

Close center back seam leaving a 4-inch opening at the waist. Clean finish opening by turning a double narrow hem to the inside and topstitching. Gather waist to fit bodice. Stitch matching center front and center backs. If necessary, hem the lower edge by turning a double narrow hem to the inside and topstitching,

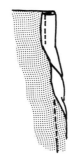

or add a lace edge by topstitching along lower edge.

❹ SNAPS: SIZE 14 MINI SNAPS

Fold under 3/4 inch along left back, press and topstitch in place. Evenly space four to five small baby snaps down center back.

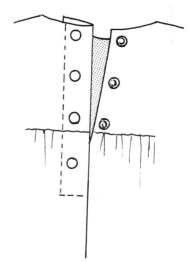

❺ OPTIONAL WAIST RIBBON

To make the gown fit more snugly, you may add a ribbon by lacing it through either round eyelet buttonholes or plain buttonholes evenly spaced around the gown at the waist line.

CHRISTENING PANTSUIT

INSTRUCTIONS

1 Fuse two 1-inch strips of interfacing to body backs to center back. With right sides together, sew center backs together leaving top 9 inches open. Finish slit on back in the same way as slit in skirt in step 3 of gown. With right sides together, sew center fronts together.

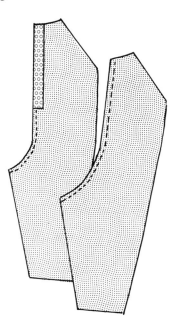

2 With right sides together, stitch raglan sleeves to fronts and back. Close inside leg seams.

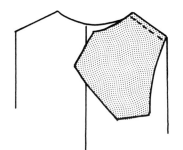

3 Elastic is applied in the same way as on gown for sleeves and legs. See step 2 in gown. Close underarm and side seams.

4 Gather neck edge to approximately 12 inches. Cut a piece of bias tape 1-1/2 inches wide or use fold-over elastic 12-1/2 inches long. Sew the short ends closed, right sides together, then turn and press right sides out. With raw edges even and right sides together, sew to neck opening. Clip curves, turn, and press. Fold to wrong side. From the right side stitch in the ditch.

5 Turn the bodies right side under and follow directions for snaps on gown step 4.

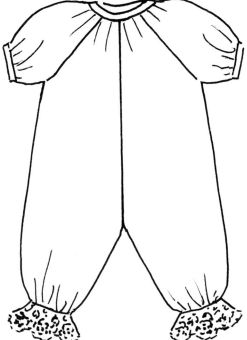

BONNET

❶ Stitch right sides together, bonnet to back, easing to fit. Repeat for lining. If adding brim for boy, interface both sections. Stitch brim, right sides together, clip curves, turn and press. Match center of brim and bonnet. Sandwich the brim between the bonnet, right sides together. Stitch the two bonnets right sides together, stitching along the lower edge leaving a 2-inch opening for turning. Turn and press well.

❷ Topstitch along all edges closing opening. For ties, cut two pieces of 1/4-inch satin ribbon. Fold under 1/2 inch on each end and stitch to bonnet corners.

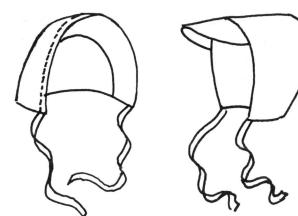

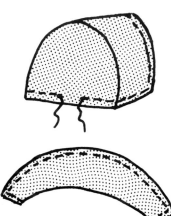

BOOTIES

*U*se pattern and directions from our baby layette in the beginning of Chapter 3. See preemie for illustrated instructions.

PART FIVE:
SIBLING GIFTS
GORILLA BABY

With all the excitement of a new baby, sometimes older sister or brother can feel left out. It is important to let them participate in all the new events a baby brings into the house. For this purpose we have created a baby gorilla (thought it would appeal better to the boys than a doll) that is just about the size of a new baby.

This gorilla needs all the care it can get and comes complete with its own baby gear. A diaper bag is very useful with built in changing pad, bib, and diapers for feeding. It even comes with a car seat that can be worn as a back pack. This will ensure hours of great play.

Note: If you want a matching set of everything, 2 yards of fabric will make the diaper bag, bib, pants, and car seat.

MATERIALS

- 3/4 yard of black polar fleece or fur
- 1/2 yard of black satin, cotton, stretch vinyl, ultra suede or ultra leather
- Large bag of polyester stuffing.
- Two safety eyes

INSTRUCTIONS

Note: If your black fabric frays, iron Easyknit™ interfacing to it prior to cutting.

1 Sew hands to arm sections and feet to leg sections.

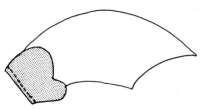

2 With right sides together, sew around arms and legs. Turn right side out.

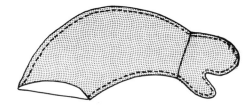

3 With right sides together, sew nose, belly button, and ears. Turn right side out and finger press. Fold nose and belly button in half with raw edges even, then baste.

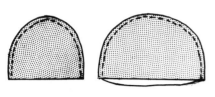

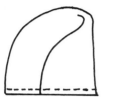

4 Sew center-face seam, enclosing nose between dots. Flatten nose out. With a buttonhole stitch, tack the center of the nose to the center of the face seam. On the sides of the face, fold eyebrow pleats downward and baste in place.

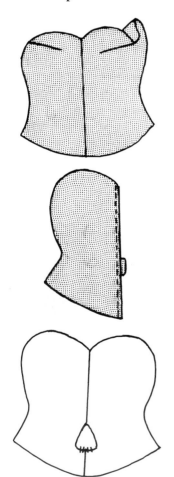

5 Sandwich belly button in between belly seam. Flatten and tack in the same way as nose.

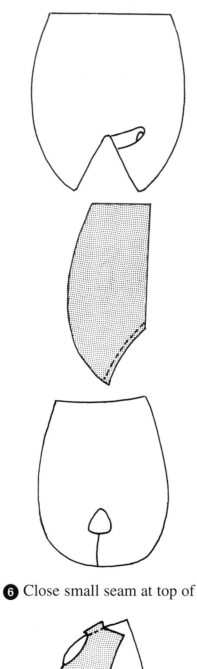

6 Close small seam at top of

armhole and seam to form leg hole. Close bottom darts.

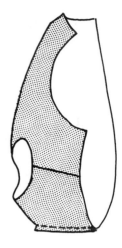

7 Sew the two body halves together, sewing from center front to center back, leaving an opening in the middle (between dots) for turning and stuffing.

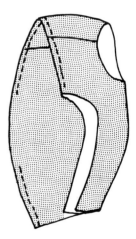

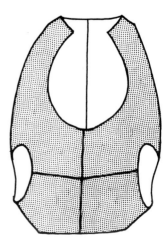

8 With right sides together, sew arms and legs in place.

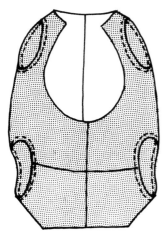

9 With right sides together, pin and sew belly in place.

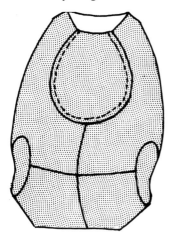

10 For head, close ear seams, sandwiching ears at the end of the ear seam.

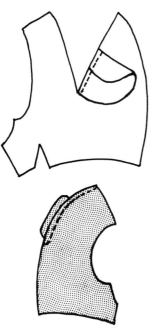

11 Close the small darts by the neck. Sew the two head halves together.

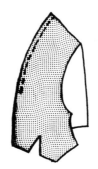

12 Sew mouth strip to chin piece. Sew chin to head.

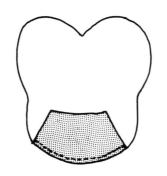

13 Pin and sew face in place. For a more Gorilla look, stitch by hand. From the right side, stitch eyebrows, then pleat fabric down toward nose. Mark and set safety eyes.

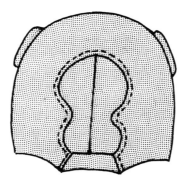

14 Attach head to body. Stuff body and head. Push stuffing down into fingers and feet, arms and legs. Close back opening.

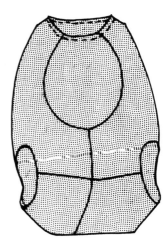

GORILLA DIAPER BAG

*T*his diaper bag holds baby bottles, clothes, and whatever else necessary. This diaper bag can be used for real babies if you just lengthen the diaper pad.

MATERIALS

- 2-1/3 yards of 1-inch fabric webbing for straps
- 1/2 yard Supplex for lining and pad
- 1 yard of interfacing
- Two snaps

CUTTING

- Cut one 14x25-inch bag piece from interfacing.
- Cut one 13x25-inch bag lining.
- Cut two 10x10-inch pockets.
- Cut three 11x20-inch diaper pad pieces, one each from fabric, interfacing, and Supplex
- Cut optional fabric straps
- Cut two 2-1/2x45-inch interface from fabric. Seam, turn, and press with seam down the center back.

INSTRUCTIONS

❶ Press top edge of pocket toward wrong side 1/2 inch. Zigzag 1/4-inch elastic over raw edge pulling firmly.

❷ Lay interfaced bag piece out, right sides up. Cut strapping in half (42 inches each). From the bottom up, position and pin straps 3-1/2 inches in from outer edge. Stop 2 inches from the top. Leave a 14-inch handle and then continue down with the strap 5 inches away from the first strap. Repeat on opposite side.

Sandwich pockets between straps. Sew each strap in place by starting from the bottom up and stop exactly 1-1/2 inches from the top bag edge. Turn and sew across strap. Continue sewing down the other side. Repeat for remaining three straps.

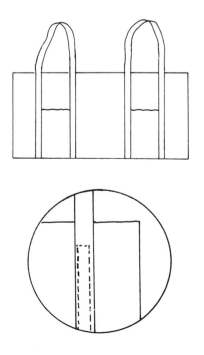

❸ With bag right sides together, sew bag closed. Repeat with bag lining. Turn bag lining so seam runs down the center back of the bag. Sew across bottom of lining.

❹ With diaper pad pieces right sides together, sew around leaving an opening at center top. Clip corners, turn and press. From the right side topstitch around pad.

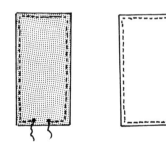

❺ With bag inside out, place diaper pad inside bag. A little of the diaper pad should stick out the bag bottom. Stitch across bag bottom twice.

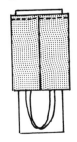

❻ Pull bag bottom apart and sew the corner to square off the bag. Repeat on lining. Take care not to catch the diaper pad.

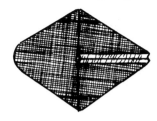

❼ Press the top edge of the bag toward the wrong side 1/2 inch and then 1 inch. With bag right side out, place lining inside bag, wrong sides together. Pin lining under press top edge of bag and then edgestitch in place.

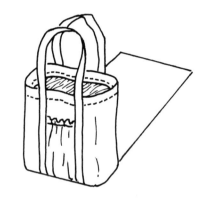

❽ For snaps, fold the diaper pad and determine the position of the snaps so the pad snaps to the bag.

GORILLA BIB

CUTTING

- ⚘ Cut one fabric.
- ⚘ Cut one lining.

INSTRUCTIONS

❶ With right sides together, sew around bib leaving an opening between dots. Clip curves well, turn, and press.

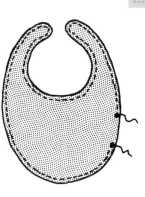

❷ From the right side, topstitch around bib closing opening. Set a snap at the neck.

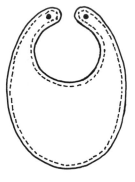

TOY CAR SEAT

*I*t looks just like a real car seat with seat belts, only this one has straps on the back and can be carried around like a back pack. It's perfect for a dolly, perfect for our gorilla baby.

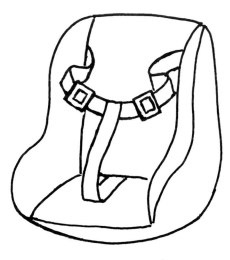

MATERIALS

- ⚘ 1 yard of fabric
- ⚘ 2-1/2 yards of 1-inch nylon webbing
- ⚘ Two parachute clips
- ⚘ Two adjustable sliders
- ⚘ Two D-rings
- ⚘ One bag of Polyester stuffing

CUTTING

- ⚘ All seam allowances 1/4 inch
- ⚘ Cut one seat bottom on fold and two car seat backs on fold.
- ⚘ Cut two back straps 22 to 25 inches long and three tabs 4 inches long.
- ⚘ Cut two front straps 7 inches long; cut 45° angle off top of each strap.
- ⚘ For seat bottom, cut one strap 10 inches and two side straps 5 inches long. Fold these in half and cut a 45° angle off the end.

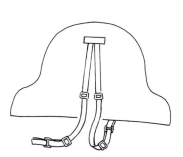

INSTRUCTIONS

❶ On one of the back car seat pieces, attach the straps as follows. Take one 4-inch piece of webbing and turn both ends under 1/4 inch. Position this on the right side of the back piece, 2-1/2 inches down from the center and pin in place (see pattern for exact location). Stick the two long straps under this tab and sew in place.

Slide the ends of the straps through a slider, threading it from back to front. Then go down through the D-ring. Coming from the back, thread it one more time through the center bar to the back again. This will make it so the straps are adjustable. Sew just the ends closed.

Note: It may be necessary to pull a lot of the strapping through the clip just so you can see what your doing and to access it for sewing.

Slide the 4-inch strap pieces through the D-rings and fold in half. Sew ends closed. Attach to bottom of seat back (see pattern for location).

❷ With right sides together, sew car-seat backs together. Turn and press.

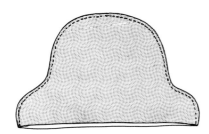

❸ Slide the top half of the parachute clips to the ends of the angled 7-inch front straps. Fold over and sew ends closed using a zigzag stitch. With front facing up, fold side of back seat inward 7 inches. Press well to form a crease. Repeat on opposite side. Place front angled straps in crease (see pattern for location) 3 inches down from the top. Edgestitch using a 1/4 inch seam, catching front seat

belt straps in seam. Backstitch over seat belts. Repeat for opposite side.

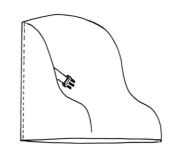

❹ Stuff the three separate compartments with stuffing. Fold two of the 4-inch straps in half, sliding a D-ring on each one. Position these at the bottom of center back 1 inch apart. Sew across the bottom to hold stuffing in place while catching the strap tabs with the D-rings.

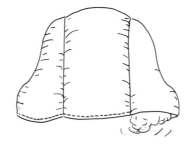

❺ Press seat bottom in half along fold. Fold one end of the 10-inch strap over 2 inches. Slide the bottom half of the parachute clips through the short pieces with angles on both ends. Sandwich theses short pieces in the folded 2-inch loop. Stitch around loop catching side straps. Position this down the center of the seat bottom.

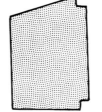
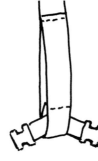

Sew to seat bottom, stopping and turning at seat fold (last few inches of strap hangs free).

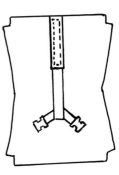

❻ Sew seat bottom to car-seat back just between the notched corners.

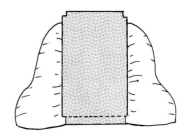

❼ Turn the corner with the seat bottom, wrapping the seat bottom around the L-shaped portion of the car seat back. The seam of the seat bottom should match the seam of the L-shaped portion. Baste first, then turn to check and make sure all the layers are caught. Sew in place. Repeat for other side.

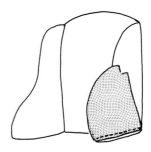

❽ Stuff the seat bottom and close the opening by hand or machine.

PEEK-A-BOO
FRIENDS

*T*hese Peek-A-Boo dolls will provide hours of sibling interaction. Older brother or sister will enjoy hiding behind these cute little dolls and then surprising baby. Baby will respond appropriately and so the game begins.

MATERIALS

- 1/3 yard of fabric
- Fabric paint
- Scraps for appliqué.

GIRL OR KITTEN PEEK A BOO

INSTRUCTIONS

1 Trace and tape pattern pieces together. Cut two bodies. The dolls are designed with two fronts.

2 Iron Wonder Under to appliqué scraps and trace appliqué parts. Iron appliqué pieces to both bodies. Satin stitch around all pieces.

3 Set stitch length smaller than normal. Place body pieces right sides together and sew around, leaving and opening at the top for turning. Clip curves and corners. Turn right side out.

4 Stuff legs and arms only. With a zipper, foot stitch across legs and arms where indicated on pattern. Fill body to neck.

Using a buttonhole stitch sew around eyes. Carefully cut away eyes, creating Peek-A-Boo areas. Continue stuffing head and around eyes. Use a pencil if necessary. Close opening. Paint faces and paws.

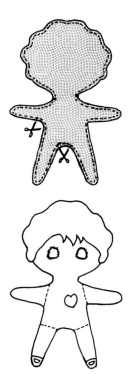

GIRL'S UNDER PANTS

*C*ut one on fold. Sew side seams. Turn top under 1/4 inch towards inside. Measure around tummy and subtract 1 inch. Cut 1/4-inch elastic to this size. Stretch and sew around inside. Turn leg opening towards inside 1/8 inch and topstitch.

Resource Listing

The fabrics used in this book came from the following sources.

THE SEWING STUDIO

11327 E. Montgomery Drive
Spokane, WA 99206
Club membership available
(800) 688-9324
FAX: (509) 926-3766

MARY'S STRETCH N SEW

8697 La Mesa Boulevard
La Mesa, CA 91941
(619) 589-8880

FIELDS FABRIC BY MAIL

1695 44th Street
Grand Rapids, MI 49508
(616) 455-4570
FAX: (616) 455-1052
www.fieldsfabrics.com

ZOODADS

PO Box 15073
Riverside, RI 02915
Fabric club available
(401) 437-2470

NOTIONS

Birch Street Clothing, Inc.
1021 S. Claremont Street
San Mateo, CA 94402
(800) 736-0854
On-Line Catalog:
www.birchstreetclothing.com
Novelty Notions, Swedish Paper, & Snaps

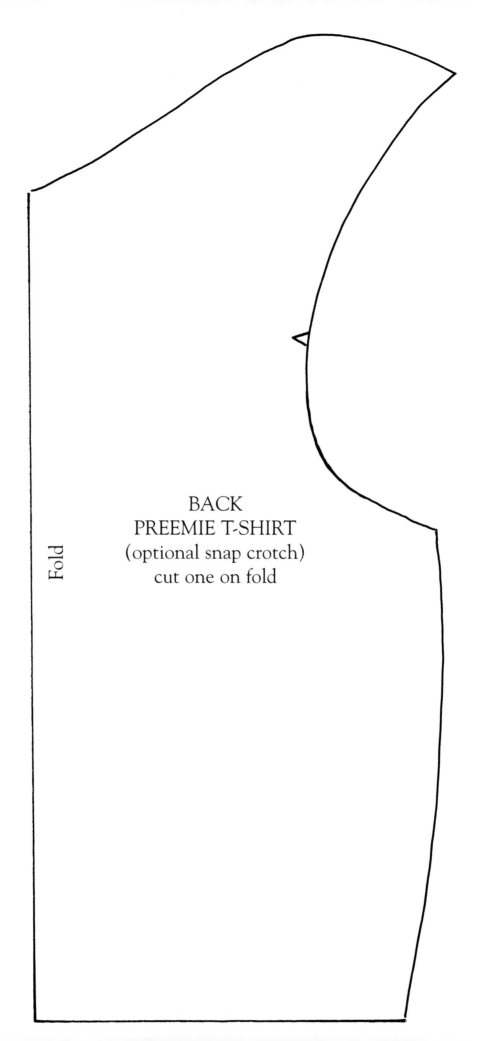

Fold

BACK
PREEMIE T-SHIRT
(optional snap crotch)
cut one on fold

BED IN A BAG LAYOUT

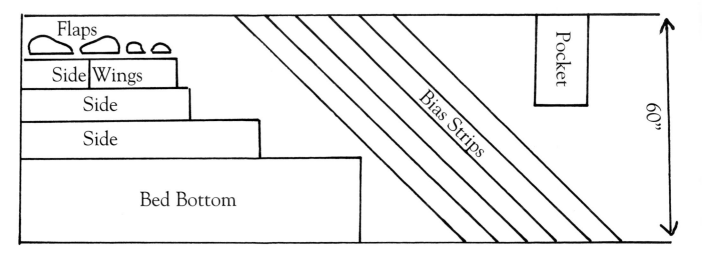

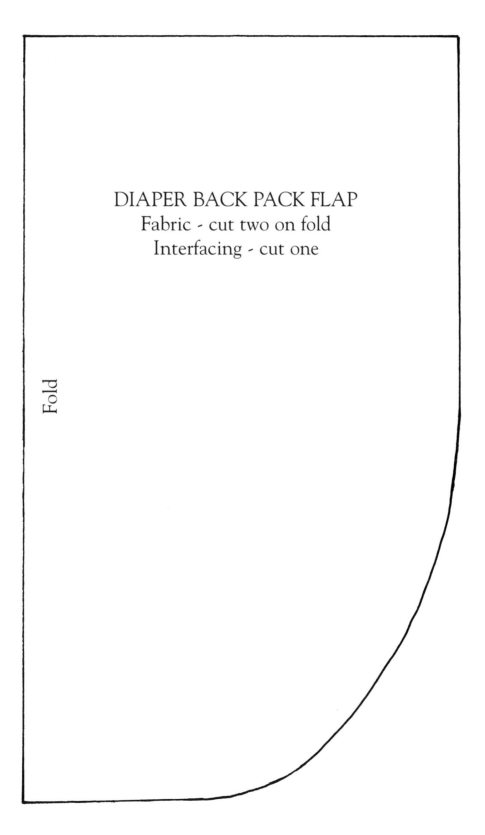

DIAPER BACK PACK FLAP
Fabric - cut two on fold
Interfacing - cut one

Fold

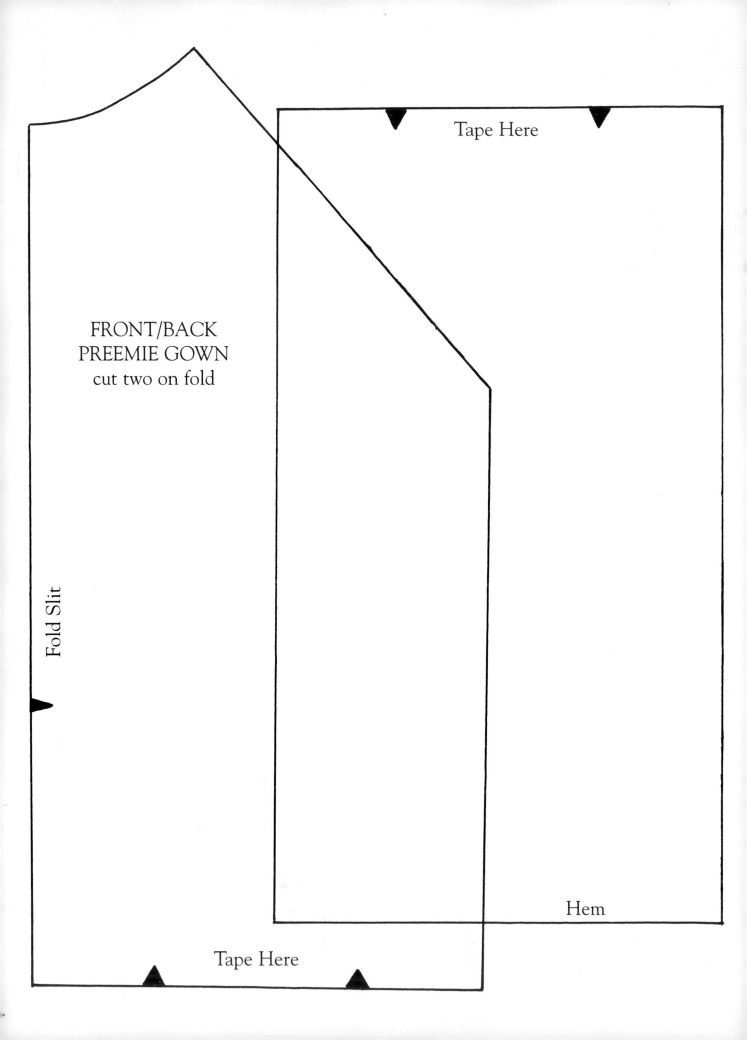

FRONT/BACK
PREEMIE GOWN
cut two on fold

Fold Slit

Tape Here

Hem

Tape Here